D1413083

*encouragement and tips*

*for stay-at-home parents*

# Celebrate
# HOME

*a Christian*

*parenting guide*

*by angie peters*

CONCORDIA PUBLISHING HOUSE • SAINT LOUIS

Some information in chapter 1 first appeared in "Homeward Bound: Six Things Every New Stay-at-Home Mom Should Know" by Angie Peters in the July/August 1996 issue of *Today's Christian Woman*.

Some information in chapter 3 first appeared in "Family Field Trips" by Angie Peters in the January/February 1997 issue of *Christian Home & School*.

Some information in chapter 3 first appeared in "Food-Time Fun" by Angie Peters in the February 1998 issue of *ParentLife*.

Some information in chapter 3 first appeared in "I'm Bored" by Angie Peters in the March 1998 issue of *ParentLife*.

Some information in chapter 7 first appeared in "Stamp Out Burnout" by Angie Peters in the March/April 1997 issue of *Christian Home & School*.

This publication may be available in braille, in large print, or on cassette tape for the visually impaired. Please allow 8 to 12 weeks for delivery. Write to the Library for the Blind, 7550 Watson Rd., St. Louis, MO 63119-4409; call 1-866-215-2455; or e-mail to blind.mission@blindmission.org.

Manufactured in the United States of America

Library of Congress Cataloging-in-Publication Data

Peters, Angie. 1964–
    Celebrate home: a survival guide for stay-at-home moms/Angie Peters.
        p. cm.
    ISBN: 0-7586-0841-1
    Mothers–United States. 2. Housewives–United States. 3. Motherhood–United States. 4. Motherhood–Religious aspects–Christianity. I. Title
HQ579.P4687    1998                                97-38687
643.7'0088'649–dc21

1   2   3   4   5   6   7   8        12   11   10   09   08   07   06   05

*For Kurt, Nick, Lindsey, and Erin*

# ACKNOWLEDGMENTS

Thanks to Peggy Kuethe for enthusiastically embracing the idea of revising this book and for everyone at CPH for being such a pleasure to work with.

Thanks to the moms who responded to my surveys and especially to my friends Donna, Susanna, and Lana for taking the time to forward the questionnaires to their friends. Because of you three I received input from dozens of women all across the country, and from one across the globe!

And as always, thanks to the people who help me stay afloat when I'm paddling in the deep end of a project, this one included. Terry, I never "coulda" done any of this without you. Tonya, Lori, Shaleen, Betsy, Debra, and Susanna, your friendship, prayers, love, notes, help with the kids, encouragement, phone calls, interest in my work, advice and hugs keep me going, body and soul.

Mom and Dad, you are everything I learned—and love—about how good home can be. Kurt, you are my home. Nick, Lindsey and Erin . . . you're the reasons I will "forever and always" celebrate home.

# TABLE OF CONTENTS

part one

## coming home

part two

*staying home*

*what about me?*

# *introduction to revised edition of celebrate home*

I stepped off the creaky elevator of the newspaper building where I had been working on the third floor writing things like profiles of local business personalities and livestock reports. Arms laden with a box of clippings, navy pumps clicking as I walked across the checkerboard-tiled lobby floor, I nodded and spoke to the receptionist before pushing through the employee exit into the glare of the April sun heralding another matchless Arkansas spring.

Grateful for the warmth inside my car—the newsroom air had been icy—I sat still for a few minutes trying to envision the full picture of what I was doing. I had quit my job—the one I had gone to college for, the one I had dreamed about landing, the one that promised to be both challenging and rewarding—to become a full time stay-at-home mom for my 16-week-old son, Nick.

Many of the questions in my mind then may be scrolling through yours now: What will I do with all that time? How will this decision change my life, my personality? How will being at home all the time affect my husband, my marriage? How will others regard me once they find out that I'm "just a mom"? Am I at risk for losing my faculties, my friends, my figure? Can we really make ends meet on one income? Will I be able to endure the material sacrifices? How long will I stay home? Will this be challenging and rewarding? Am I doing the right thing? *Will this really make a difference?*

Now—15 years later—I can't answer all of these questions for you, but I can let you know how they were answered for me and for many other women who made the u-turn from the working world to the home front. That's the kind of information you'll find in the pages of this book.

I wrote the first version of *Celebrate Home* in 1998, when very few materials on bookshelves, in magazine racks, on television, or on the Internet supported or encouraged moms at home. Articles about dressing for success and asking for a raise were far more common than articles about dressing on a budget or asking for advice on teething. A woman was likely to find more book titles telling her how to multitask at work than how to do fourteen things at once at home.

So I wrote a book designed to step in as a career coach, of sorts, for rookie stay-at-home moms. I hoped it would fill a void that very much needed to be filled.

Today, as the "information age" explodes on all fronts, that void isn't as cavernous. Thankfully, many more books, Web sites, articles, ministries, and organizations are equipping and encouraging us in our at-home careers. That's a good thing because more of us—moms and dads alike—are staying home to raise our kids now than then. In 2000, the U.S. Census Bureau reported the first significant decline in the number of new moms in the labor force; the number decreased from 59 percent to 55 percent between 1998 and 2000. While that drop, according to one article, had statistics-trackers "scratching their heads," it made perfect sense to those of us who were at home enjoying fringe benefits of a career that had indeed proved loaded with both challenges and rewards.

Although more and more resources for stay-at-home moms have hit the shelves and been posted on the Net through the years, this small book—written by a frazzled but focused mom because she loved her new job so much she wanted to make the transition easier for others—has continued to hold its own in the bookstores. But like any of us, the book was due for a freshening up. My publisher and I decided to pull it off the shelf, give its cover and its content a makeover, and re-release it. I think you'll be pleased with the results.

In this new edition, you'll find most of the same information that made *Celebrate Home* a cheering squad, a checklist, a coffee break, and a comfort zone for stay-at-home moms. But you'll also find a few changes:

✳ It's updated where needed (I think you'll be happy to see that I no longer refer to the Internet as a "new and exciting tool").

✳ It includes material about issues concerning women who continue to stay home beyond the preschool years.

✳ It features fresh insights from new and from seasoned mothers at home.

✳ It includes a new feature called "on-the-job hazard" to alert you to some of the potential pitfalls of stay-at-home motherhood and help you avoid them.

✳ It concludes with information-packed appendices that will be handy when you need practical or spiritual help in a hurry.

Now, back to that list of questions crowding into my thoughts after my final day at work. See the last question, the one about whether staying at home would really make a difference? I'd like to answer that one for you here since I have the benefit of viewing my own career change through the wide-angled lens of the years that have passed. My son, who was just four years old when I started writing the first edition of this book, is now in the midst of what might be his final four years in our home (that is, if he goes away to college, and I admit that at this point I'm tightening the apron strings and lobbying for the local university campus!). His younger sister, Lindsey, was a toddler busy with blocks and baby dolls when I was editing the first draft of that manuscript; she's now a tween-ager busy with school-work and friends. Their baby sister, Erin, who wasn't even on our agenda in those first edition days, is now a bright-eyed, question-spouting kindergartner. I can find no words powerful enough to express to you, Mom, how quickly these years have flown. Has my staying home really mattered? My answer is yes. Every minute I've spent rocking and reading, holding and handling, training and teaching, discipling and disciplining, laughing with and loving my kids—in short, staying home with them—has made a difference. A big one.

# introduction

> Even the sparrow finds a home, and the swallow a nest for herself, where she may lay her young, at Your altars, O LORD of hosts, my King and my God. Psalm 84:3

When I first came home, elated at the prospect of being my wide-eyed, black-haired, 4-month-old's mom all day, every day, I knew the opportunity to do this had been a gift handed straight from heaven. Daily life sprawled in front of me with watercolor clarity in a collage of hand-knitted booties, rocking-chair lullabies, and the everlasting scent of baby powder.

Using these lofty expectations for a compass, I didn't give myself permission to dislike anything about my new job as the months began to roll by. If I started to feel lonely or isolated because none of my neighbors were at home during the day, I told myself I must be crazy to complain when I had obviously landed the best job in town. If I struggled with the blues after turning a friend down for lunch because I didn't have the extra cash, I told myself I was being selfish for wanting to have my chicken salad croissant and eat it too.

But just after Lindsey was born, after Nick had started to talk but before he was potty trained, a friend invited me to sign up for a MOPS (Mothers of Preschoolers) program. It met one Friday morning a month at a local church.

I knew it would probably feel good to get out of the house, so I said, "Sure." It was incredibly hard to get an infant, a toddler, and myself out of bed, fed, dressed, packed, and out the door by 8 A.M. that first Friday. But when I got there, I was thrilled to discover that about 150 other moms had gone to the same trouble as I that morning just to be there. Most of those moms, I learned, were also staying at home.

I couldn't believe that this many women had chosen to trek down the same "less chosen" path as I. They, too, were clearly committed to stay-at-home motherhood. But they, too, got lonely. They, too, had to watch their money—every penny of it. In a world that seemed to revolve around careers, clothes, and money, I found a bunch of women whose lives centered, like mine, around babies, diaper coupons, and nursery rhymes.

Many of us, quite honestly, simply were neither prepared nor equipped to meet the unique set of challenges abruptly introduced by our gutsy move into a stay-at-home, one-income lifestyle. Even those of us who could balance a mega-dollar budget at our former, "real" jobs were finding it difficult to manage the checking account for our growing households on our decreased income. Those of us who could smooth the ruffled feathers of even the angriest customers were having trouble calming our cranky, teething toddlers. We could coordinate important meetings—from setting the agenda to putting together the Power Point presentation—but we were at a loss for ideas for stimulating, educational, fun activities for our little ones seven days a week, 52 weeks a year.

We performed our "real" jobs with skill and confidence because we had been educated and trained to do those jobs. But negotiating that path from the corporate world to the domestic required us to spend our days doing things many of us never expected, planned, or learned how to spend our days doing.

At each MOPS meeting, we cheered new births with a pack of newborn pink or blue diapers "pre-loaded" by committed planners with a Bible verse hand-picked to inspire tired moms during wee-hour changes. We celebrated just-found-out-about pregnancies with a symbolic pack of saltines to help ward off the morning sickness. We hung on every word of advice from our seasoned teaching leaders who took their role as Titus 2:4 women to heart by answering God's call to teach the younger women. We prayed together for the young lives we are trying to shape, for our marriages, for our homes, and for ourselves. And we cried together at the close of each nine-month session as we said good-bye to the moms who wouldn't be returning the next fall because they had "graduated" from preschool motherhood as their youngest ones headed off for first grade.

We celebrated their success in surviving the preschool years. We longingly wondered how that independence they were regaining as their children grew would feel when we got there. But most of all we grieved with them for the all-too-quick passage of the baby days.

Each MOPS meeting left me feeling energized, equipped, and excited about being a mom. I always looked forward to the next month's gathering. Other moms voiced my feelings as they drifted out the doors, infant carriers and diaper bags in tow.

I believe those meetings became so important to all of us because they reminded us that we are not alone in our journey as mothers at home. That's why I began writing this book—to capture the sense of comfort and community moms at home get from gathering with other moms at home. We need someone to speak to us, not from the pages of a glossy magazine that show us what our lives should be like, but from where we are— taking care of kids (both ours and, often, a couple of extras too), cleaning house, trying to grab a few minutes to read the Bible or a daily devotional, making do with what we've got, working at our churches, cooking din- ner, picking up blocks, letting the hem out of a pair of pants, taking cupcakes to a school party, balancing our checkbooks, and buying groceries with a creeper nap- ping in the shopping cart and a toddler waddling beside it.

We need practical ideas. We need a plan. We need advice. We need encouragement. We need spiritual guidance. We need to know how to make the absolute most of these days we have been given to spend as our little ones' number one caregivers. Because we know, and everybody keeps telling us, "These years will be gone before you know it."

I hope *Celebrate Home* fills that order. I've researched existing literature, surveyed hundreds of stay-at-home moms and interviewed dozens of others, and collected other bits and pieces of information that I thought might help mothers who have decided to make their homes their primary workplaces for the next few months, seasons, or years.

The desire to be a homemaker, to be the principal caretaker of young children, is admirable. But the daily tasks of this job require a humble heart and a realization that God has entrusted us with a unique calling, a wondrous gift. As we set about "celebrating home," we will find that God is at work in our lives to guide us as we establish routines, reach milestones, and personally define stay-at-home parenthood. His presence is very real in all that we do in our daily lives. No, we are never alone in our journey.

My prayer is that this book will help you quickly find your definition of career parenthood so you can discover lots of reasons to celebrate home with confidence, faith, love, and God's grace every day.

# part one

# coming home

"I have learned in whatever situation I am to be content. I know how to be brought low, and I know how to abound. In any and every circumstance, I have learned the secret of facing plenty and hunger, abundance and need. I can do all things through Him who strengthens me."

Philippians 4:11–13

# chapter one

# more than an adventure —it's your job

> By wisdom a house is built, and by understanding it is established; by knowledge the rooms are filled with all precious and pleasant riches. Proverbs 24:3–4

Visions of the homes of Samantha "Bewitched" Stevens and Carol "Brady Bunch" Brady danced through my head as I pulled out of the employee parking lot after my last day of work as a features writer for the local paper.

The fruits of my family's newly adopted lifestyle, I speculated, would include quality time, all the time, with my then 4-month-old son, Nick, and his future brothers and sisters; nutritious, delicious meals on the table each morning, noon, and night; an immaculate home, decorated exquisitely; and enough time to finally do all those things I had been meaning to do: learn to sew, volunteer, paint, write a book . . .

After a few weeks, however, the time that had stretched before my eyes as expansively as the Grand Canyon shrank into a trickle about as wide as the stream of spilled milk trailing across the kitchen floor.

I couldn't manage to keep the diaper pail emptied, much less vacuum the entire house. Dinner, I hated to admit, still included those heat-em-ups we relied upon so heavily when I worked outside the home. By the time I did have a few minutes to call my own, I barely had enough energy to call a sympathetic friend and confide my failures. "What," I asked her, "am I doing wrong?"

Quicker than a toddler can knock over a potted plant on freshly cleaned carpet, she pointed out three things:

1. Samantha Stevens had a magic nose.

2. Carol Brady had Alice.

3. Neither of these women, as far as we in TV audienceland know, took their mothering responsibilities any more seriously than the plans they were making for their latest dinner party.

Since magic noses obviously don't run in my family and our lopped-off household income could not support the salary of a full-time, live-in, aproned helper, I realized that I might just have to work hard at becoming a successful stay-at-home mom. Round-filing my two-dimensional, television-family-of-my-childhood expectations, I began to tackle my new "job" as realistically as I would any paying job: I determined to learn exactly what it was I was supposed to be doing and to learn how to do my new job well.

# YOUR JOB DESCRIPTION:
## WHAT ARE YOU SUPPOSED TO DO ALL DAY?

If you had just landed a new job out in the "real" world, the scenario on your first day might go something like this: You arrive at work, well dressed, on time, and eager, but nervous. Your new boss greets and welcomes you, handing over a copy of your new job description as she shows you around the office. She introduces you to coworkers, whom she instructs to lend you a hand when you look confused. Leading you to your work area, she tosses onto your desk a set of printed instructions outlining your first assignment.

You know you can handle this assignment, not only because she has carefully run through it but also because she has let you know that during your first days you will have her support—and that of your colleagues—as you learn your way around the office and become familiar with your new responsibilities.

Now, flash back to the home front. Unfortunately,

we moms don't have a supervisor to show us the ropes as we learn about our new job. We don't have the luxury of a printed list of job requirements to turn to when we wake up each morning, an entire day facing us. All we have is our own set of intangible goals we must somehow reach while pouring cereal, wiping noses, calling repair people, chaperoning class trips, and cleaning house.

Our parenting and homemaking goals vary as widely as the paths we'll need to take to reach them, but a great step toward getting your bearings is to make two lists.

### 1. The Big Picture

Think about long-term goals relating to your role as a parent, your children, your

families, your personal dreams. Think back to the reasons you quit work in the first place. For example, when I've just told Erin, 5, that I can't read a book because I'm folding clothes, or when I get angry at Lindsey for trying to get my attention while I'm talking to my friend on the phone, I have to remind myself that I didn't quit my job to clean house. I don't stay home so I can talk on the phone. I don't stay home so I can watch home decorating shows every afternoon. I am here to raise my children.

### 2. The Day-to-Day Details

Once you have a sense of your family's big priorities, get down to the nitty gritty. Ask yourself what matters most to you regarding your everyday expectations. Be honest with yourself as you prioritize your activities—this isn't a report for the boss or a test or quiz. If home-baked cookies are a higher priority for you than mopping the floor, write it down. If a dirty sink makes you crazy, put "keep a clean sink" at the top of your list.

These lists will form the closest thing to a job description you'll ever get, so post them on the fridge, in the front of your day planner, or in your Bible because they will help you at least get the first things done first. That way, at the end of each day, you won't regret not having cleaned the fridge because you'll realize that it was, indeed, more important to you to have made toilet-paper-roll dinosaurs with your toddler.

# NEEDED: QUALIFIED APPLICANTS

Now that you've identified your goals and priorities, let's backtrack a little to look at another aspect of this job you've landed: qualifications. Which characteristics can you develop that will help you do this new job well?

Certainly some of the following traits desired in applicants for a variety of jobs advertised in our local paper on a recent Sunday are traits helpful in a mothering career:

# help wanted!

- ○ People skills
- ○ Leadership skills
- ○ Innovative thinking
- ○ Self-starting
- ○ Ability to work independently
- ○ Creativity
- ○ Ability to work in fast-paced environment
- ○ Mental acuity
- ○ Organizational skills
- ○ Communication skills
- ○ Ability to learn new tasks quickly

But the people-raising business requires even more powerful characteristics of the members of its workforce. Some of the following terms might be included on an application for mothering, if there were such a thing:

Faith
Wisdom
Discernment
Domestic prowess
Patience
Humor
Culinary creativity
Tenderheartedness
Mercy
Frugality
Compassion
Abundant energy
Sensitivity

*do you have?*

Budgeting prowess
Perseverance
Emotional stamina
Integrity
Positive outlook
Listening skills
Adaptability
Tact
Diligence
Kindness
Love
Forgiveness

*do you have?*

If this seems like a daunting list of qualifications, you're right; it is! Daunting, but—thanks to the Lord—do-able, if we concentrate on becoming the right women for the job.

## LEARNING NEW SKILLS

I had always dreamed of becoming a freelance writer and editor. I majored in English, took that job as a newspaper writer right out of college, and, after quitting that job to become a stay-at-home mom, developed a home-based word processing service. My income did little more than pay for a few packages of diapers or an occasional dinner out, but I knew the endeavor was helping me to gain experience, develop contacts, and most important, it was allowing me to do the thing I loved to do: work with words, even if I was just typing words other people had written. But one day, I saw a help-wanted listing that made my heart race. "Wanted: Writer's assistant. Published author seeks part-time assistance in manuscript preparation. Some research." I popped my résumé in the mail before Lindsey had emptied her second bottle of formula for the day.

God's grace worked in a way that allowed my qualifications to add up to make me just the kind of assistant this writer was seeking. I couldn't have dreamed up better circumstances, even if I had tried (see Ephesians 3:20). As it turned out, not only was this person a reputable, published author, but he also "happened" to be a Christian. He "happened" to write Christian books for a Christian publishing company. He "happened" to live less than 10 minutes from my home. He "happened" to want help only occasionally and from someone who would do the work at his or her home. And he "happened" to be a member of the church my husband and I had just begun visiting. Some would call this "fate," "coincidence," or "luck." I know better. God was at work.

I would, I learned during our first interview, be reading research material onto tapes (because of the writer's failing vision), handling occasional correspondence, and editing and proofreading manuscripts after having entered those manuscripts into the . . . computer.

Oh, no. Not a computer!

I somehow managed to graduate from high school and college without ever taking a computer course. I had done all my previous work on a word processor that was little more than a fancy typewriter with a memory. The prospect of being expected to use a computer was as scary to me as sentence diagramming might be to a math major.

But I knew I wasn't about to say, "Sorry, can't do." Not when it was so clear that this opportunity was part of God's perfectly orchestrated plan for me and my family. So I became the right person for the job by taking a computer course to learn the skills I needed. Within a few weeks, I was navigating my way through directories and files with ease.

What I'm getting at is this: As a mom, you have landed this great job with loads of responsibility, great pay (in intangible and eternal terms, anyway), and fantastic fringe benefits (you can't beat the dress code and the flexible hours!). But since you may not have expected to end up making your kids and your home your career, your list of outstanding skills may sketch a picture more corporate than domestic, more material than maternal. You might have to work at getting the hang of the skills in areas in which you fall short.

How can you go about mastering practical domestic or parenting skills? By tapping into the wide variety of resources available. For example, if you're not confident that you're giving your family a nutritious diet, go to the library or bookstore for help. If reading isn't your cup of tea, try videotapes or DVDs. As you glance through monthly house and home magazines, keep an eye out for useful articles. And take advantage of the Internet. In addition to giving at-home moms much-needed contact with other moms all across the globe, the online world offers fast and easy access to all kinds of information—from homeschooling and medical reports to movie reviews and kids' crafts. (See Appendix C for a detailed list of resources for stay-at-home parents.)

# LOOKING TO GOD

We know we can become the kind of moms God wants us to be because countless godly moms have come before us. We can read about many of these women in the Bible. For example, consider the virtuous woman described in Proverbs 31:10–31. This Bible-times mom was, among other things, a wise, creative, patient, good, generous, kind, diligent, frugal, and

# On the Job Hazard!

### Getting Hooked on the Net

While the Internet may be just about the next best thing to baby wipes, there's one hitch: It's easy to spend too much time surfing, browsing, and chatting and not enough time parenting. For example, one mom says she had to give up online chat rooms, bulletin boards, and forums because she found herself "spending way too much time soapboxing about staying home and not enough time with my kids." So when you log on, consider setting the kitchen timer!

responsible woman. And yes, hers would be some pretty big sandals to fill, especially on a day-to-day basis. This woman didn't have electricity, reclosable disposable diapers, a butcher shop, plumbing, a mini-van or SUV, precooked chicken nuggets, a sewing machine, a microwave oven, or Wal-Mart a block away. She didn't even have a box of Calgon to sprinkle into her bath water to take her away after she unbraided her hair, shed her sweaty robe, and kicked off those dusty sandals at the end of her long, hot day. Yet she rose above the exhausting and mundane details of her life with a grace and beauty that compelled her children to call her blessed, her husband to be known far and wide, and her entire community to benefit from her generosity and sweet spirit.

How did Mrs. Virtuous Woman manage her mission of mothering so masterfully? By keeping her mind and heart tuned in to God's constant love and mercy. You and I can do that too. All we have to do is ask for some heavenly help.

One day when Nick was about 4, I stood inside the patio door watching him try to hoist his still baby-fat, compact, 2-year-old sister up and into her baby swing. For a good 20 minutes he tried. First he reached around her from behind, his arms under hers, clasping his hands in front of her chest and lifted her off the ground. But he just couldn't figure out how to transfer his squirming bundle into the swing. Then Nick tried another strategy. He grabbed her from the front, nearly falling over backward because she sweetly tried to help him by thrusting herself into his arms.

As I watched my son nearly wear himself out, I had to restrain myself from going out to help. Instead, I decided to simply watch the mini-drama unfold. But I kept thinking, *he could save himself so much trouble if he'd just ask me for help.* Then I realized I had perhaps caught a glimpse of what God must see us doing every day as we try so hard to do so many things without even thinking about asking for His help. I'll leave the preaching to our pastors, but from one mom to another, He can make our jobs as mothers and wives and daughters and friends and housekeepers and carpool drivers and nurses and play dough makers and money managers so much easier. If we'll only ask.

"Ask, and it will be given to you; seek, and you will find; knock, and it will be opened to you. For everyone who asks receives, and the one who seeks finds, and to the one who knocks it will be opened." (Matthew 7:7)

If any of you lacks wisdom, let him ask
God  who gives generously to all without
reproach, and it will be given him. (James 1:5)

Call to Me and I will answer you,
and will tell you great and hidden things
that you have not known. (Jeremiah 33:3)

# LIVING IN LIGHT OF YOUR CALLING

In doing the research to revise this book, I sent out dozens of questionnaires to mothers across the country asking for their input on various aspects of their job as stay-at-home moms. But my drive to professionalize motherhood by using working world terminology didn't seem quite right to one precious mom. To a question I had phrased, "What were some of the most difficult adjustments you had to make in your new job as a mother at home?" she tactfully responded: "I see my role not as a job, but as a privilege and as a calling."

Ouch! I feel the same way; I just failed to make sure that message came across in the survey. So I want to state loudly and clearly right here: Motherhood is indeed a privilege and a calling! And, thankfully, when we think of this fact as we consider the qualifications we might need to be the best moms we can be, we know we can always count on God's promise that He will never abandon those whom He has called. Perhaps you can identify with Moses as God called him to lead His people out of Egypt. Faced with the overwhelmingly complex chore of raising children and the responsibility of shaping their minds and hearts in a way that prepares them to meet all the challenges they will face in their lives, we may feel like saying to God, as Moses did, "Who am I, that You have called me to do this job? I feel so unqualified, unskilled, unprepared, inadequate." But when our confidence wanes, we can be empowered by God's answer: "Certainly I will be with you" (Exodus 3:11–12).

Even beyond that promise, God backs up His words with actions. He told Moses exactly what to say, gave him the tools with which to perform the miracles, and gave him a helper in Aaron. Likewise, God reinforces His promise to be with us through giving us access to His Word, which is full of specific instructions as vital and relevant to the life of a housewife and mother of today as to a Jewish woman in ancient times.

"I have come to realize that without Christ, raising children would be a fear-controlling responsibility," says Leslie, whose five kids range in ages from 2 to 22. "The Bible has truly been a guidebook in all aspects of child-rearing." Along with the guidelines Scripture gives us as parents, it offers us the peace of knowing that when we (and our children) fail to follow, we can be forgiven in Christ.

## LEARNING IT TAKES TIME

During the first months and even the first few years of stay-at-home mothering, it's important not to expect instant results in this new career you've chosen. In fact, leaving one identity, a career-oriented one, behind and attaching to a new, child-oriented identity seems to come for most women gradually rather than suddenly. It's like breaking in new shoes: Sometimes you just have to walk around in them for a few days before they begin to fit just right.

Kelly, who left her job as a recruiting coordinator for a law firm more than five years ago to stay at home with her children, says it took her quite some time to settle into her new role. "It was definitely a 'surrendering' process that took almost two years (just before my second daughter was born), until I truly felt comfortable in the motherhood role," she says.

Comforting to keep in mind as we work to become the new women for the vocation our heavenly Father, has called us to is that our heavenly Father is in the business of working breathtaking transformations in the lives of people who want to work toward His goals. Certainly if He could turn meek Moses into the mighty leader He needed to be to lead His people, He can transform a domestically challenged mother like me into the mighty mom He wants me to be to raise part of His next generation! As we can see in Philippians 1:6, God will keep shaping us, perfecting us, until the Last Day when He has us exactly how He wants us: "And I am sure of this, that He who began a good work in you will bring it to completion at the day of Jesus Christ." What a promise to lean on when we feel like we don't know what we're doing!

# LETTING GO OF THE WHEEL

The rules have changed. When you were in the workplace, you did this and got paid that. You put together a report and got the satisfaction of seeing a neatly typed, collated project inserted in the impressive-looking folder. You made a speech and got a pat on the back from a colleague. You met your sales quota and got the peace of mind that the boss wouldn't be on your case anymore. You did x and got y. You were in control, if not of your destiny, then at least of your days.

But the equation has changed. When you're parenting at home, nothing guarantees that y will follow x. Too many interruptions keep you from completing x to begin with. If you do manage to complete x, there's usually no one around to give you the y. No bonuses for baby rocking. No certificates of recognition for efficient diaper-bag packing. No employee of the month parking spot for teaching your son to chew with his mouth closed. No brownie points for getting lunch ready today before the kids got cranky and without any spills.

"I do miss the feedback of a job well done," says Liz, who has been at home with her daughter for 11 years. She left her job as a technical communicator and was attending graduate school when she made the career switch.

"When you're a mom, especially with infants, you just change diapers and feed them," adds Leslie. "That's all you do. Tend to their needs and there's no end to it. You don't say, 'Well at this point I'm going to be finished with that.' . . . It's really incredibly frustrating."

"The biggest challenge has been my own perception of my worth and competence," admits Kelly, mother of two. "This is the most difficult position I have ever held. The responsibility is huge! If I fail to do a good job, my family is directly impacted. When you are the main component in the rearing of your children, you are the one who is responsible for their well-being. There is no daycare to blame, no nanny to replace—it's just you!"

There are no easy answers for dealing with the frustration wrought by this kind of drastic change of course midgame. But if you can let go of the wheel and turn your days into a celebration of life with your kids—interruptions and all—the Lord will honor your commitment by adjusting your needs to be satisfied with a new set of rewards. That reward may be as simple as a sticky kiss instead of brownie points with the boss, but that sticky kiss can deliver an inner peace beyond any raise you ever got. And a major factor in that peace is the knowledge that we aren't the perfect parent—God is. We can know that every time we feel frustrated because we fall short of the standard we've set for ourselves, we are forgiven.

You may not be getting feedback in the form of an annual performance review, but "overall, having the feedback from a child who adores you is pretty awesome," says Liz.

# Chapter 2

# your number one colleague: marriage matters

> Two are better than one, because they have a good reward for their toil. For if they fall, one will lift up his fellow. But woe to him who is alone when he falls and has not another to lift him up! Ecclesiastes 4:9–10

" . . . And when youth has passed, may they be found then, as now, still hand in hand, still thanking God for each other. May they serve You happily, and faithfully, until one shall lay the other into the arms of God."

Nineteen Christmases, three pregnancies, five moves, 11 vehicles, nine soccer seasons, four dance recitals, 22 class projects, and 7,789 loads of laundry have tumbled through our lives since the pastor voiced that sweet wedding blessing over our bowed heads as we clutched each other's hands in a church full of friends and family one rainy May Saturday night.

At the time, Rev. Logue probably had no idea what an impact his tender blessing was to have on that 21-year-old girl who was leaving the security and comfort of her mom and dad's home to blaze her own trail in the unknown wilderness of marriage and homebuilding. Events both mundane and sensational have knocked on our cabin door through the years, threatening, at times, to flip-flop our priorities and minimize the significance of our marriage. I've echoed that prayer so often it has become permanently etched in my heart. The words remind me that Kurt and I—our relationship, not our circumstances—are the perpetual event that is our marriage. It was just us then—two kids reverently and nervously holding hands before God in that sanctuary full of celebrants. And it's just us now—two parents clinging to the stability and familiarity of each other's hands as we feel our way through the labyrinth of challenges that guide us through this people-raising adventure.

If we don't do what it takes *now* to keep our marriage sturdy, our love affair alive, we might have to work double-time to repair the damage *then*, when we reach our later years clutching the comfort of each other's hands as we witness the bittersweet milestones—first dates, graduations, marriages—that will carry each of our children further from our care and closer to independence.

So how do we keep our partnership stable, our

romance kindled? Is that even possible, given the shift in our work roles, the nightly feedings, a 15-pound weight gain (I won't say whose), tag-team rampages of chicken pox, weekly crises ranging from finding jeans to fit an in-between-sizes preteen before the big party Friday night to searching for a missing lovey-bear for baby before bedtime, and a steady stream of unexpected budget-busting expenses? Absolutely!

**Protect the partnership.** We can guard our marriages (read Malachi 2:15–16) by offering an unhesitating "yes" to any activity that enhances, protects or strengthens our relationship and an uncompromising "no" to any activity that can potentially undermine, damage or even destroy it.

**Reconnect regularly.** One night at supper, Kurt mentioned getting approval on a project at work that I had no idea he had been working on. Our lines of communication had become so clogged with the activities of the past few weeks that we hadn't been connecting through any real conversation more meaningful than "What do you want for dinner?" "Will you  be home in time to take Lindsey to her soccer practice?" or "I need you to pick up milk and lunchmeat on your way home from work." We hadn't been grabbing any time to reconnect at the end of each night or even at the end of each week and now we were seeing the results. Although we weren't exactly teetering on the brink of an empty and lifeless marriage, I knew this was a red flag calling for quick action. All we needed to repair this communication breakdown was a date night. We needed to shift our focus from family, friends and the calendar to each other. Here are some other ways to stay in sync with your mate in the craziness of a busy family's activities:

**Get up 30 minutes earlier** each morning to chat over a cup of hot tea or coffee.

**Exercise together**—walk three times a week, play a set of tennis once a month, fish, camp, go for a bike ride . . .

**Sit on the front step or back deck to watch your children play together.** The kids feel they have your undivided attention but they don't realize you're snatching a real conversation with one another at the same time.

**Hold hands** every chance you get.

**Linger at the dinner table after the kids have drifted away to play.** The dishes aren't going anywhere.

**Don't let the kids derail your stolen moments.** A snuggly conversation on the couch on a rainy Sunday afternoon, a Saturday night rerun of the movie you saw on your first date, a spontaneous snack of cookies and milk at the kitchen counter while the kids are getting ready for bed—these are moments you don't plan. And children, at times, seem to be designed to destroy these moments with demands of all shapes and sizes. Be marriage-minded

mates, and without taking your eyes off each other,
say, "Not now, we're in the middle of something; we'll
take care of you in a little bit." In a world where
marriages are falling apart all around our kids, this
message of solidarity will comfort them whether they
realize it or not by letting them know your marriage
is a permanent fixture in their lives and that it's one
you take seriously.

**Spend time with other adults.** You don't have to
be alone on a date to connect. Sometimes going to a
party or on a double date with friends can help you
enjoy each other just as well. A fun evening with
friends makes climbing into the car alone together
afterward seem even more intimate.

**Try something new together.** I was completely
flabbergasted when my mom mentioned over the
phone one day a few years ago that she and Dad had
been looking at houseboats. "To buy?" I gasped. This
mother and father who had never camped in my
whole life were going to live for two or three days,
maybe even a week or two, at a time, in nothing
more than a floating camper? But a couple of months
later, my dad, proudly wearing his new captain's hat,
was deftly easing a beautiful houseboat away from the
dock as my mom, the first mate, adeptly maneuvered
the ropes. I looked on, impressed, and imagined what
fun and memories they must have made as they
learned this new hobby together.

**Worship together.** An important part of your
God-given vocation as parents is to bring up your
children in the community of believers. It's equally
important in your God-given vocation as wife or

husband to maintain your marriage in that community. Sit side-by-side in the pew. Kneel shoulder-to-shoulder. Pray together. You'll walk out of the service and into the rest of the week as partners in faith and parenting.

**Mark down memories.** Remember when you were first dating and first married, how you would save a ticket stub from that special concert to paste into your scrapbook, hang snapshots of your sun-kissed honey at the lake on your bathroom mirror, or get misty-eyed when the radio played your song? Then the kids came along and now it's ticket stubs from the circus that you save to stuff into the baby book, snapshots of your baby's first gummy smile that you affix to every vertical surface of your home, and lullabies you sang to your eight-year-old when he was a baby that call up the lump in your throat. Your focus has understandably shifted, but take time to travel down those memory lanes you share. Look at old snapshots together, reminisce about the good old days, and mentally file away funny stories and mementos of your current life together. Press the rose he brought you last week because he knew you'd had a rough day, and tuck away, don't toss, the coffee-stained reminder to pick up the dry-cleaning he wrote last week that had a P.S. that gave you a spring in your step all day: "You're the best. I love you."

**Look ahead.** We may be so busy we can hardly see beyond the next load of laundry so it's important to touch base from time to time to talk about the big picture. Have you always said you'd like another baby but things have gotten so busy with the kids you have you just haven't stopped long enough to discuss it?

Did you and your husband expect to have made that trip to Europe by the time you reached your mid-30s? Has he always said he'd really like to go into business for himself one day? Is it time to consider how to help one of your parents whose health is failing? Have you always wanted to start a home business? If you don't schedule some unstructured time together to allow these topics to surface, they may not get discussed until the opportunity has passed or until a decision must be made in haste or under pressure. Lots of times these kinds of conversations allow you to revise your plans and dreams as circumstances change.

# MOM STAYING HOME
## DISRUPTS DAD'S WORLD TOO

Most discussions about and among at-home moms center on two subjects: mothering and children. Because your husband, or so it seems, is the one whose life is least visibly disrupted by the birth of a child and your shift from workplace to home, rarely is much attention paid to his vantage point. While you're concentrating on new priorities and adjusting to the about-face in how you're now spending your days and thoughts, he's heading for work each morning, wearing the same clothes, seeing the same people, doing the same things he has been doing for months or years.

What we don't often hear discussed is that your conversion from office to home does disrupt your husband's world, and in more ways than you might realize. Here are a few questions, phrased from his perspective, that might help you identify and address some of the concerns of a husband of stay-at-home mom.

# IS THIS THE WOMAN I MARRIED?

Not only is your husband continually adjusting to the ever-changing pressures and responsibilities of parenthood, he is also adapting to being married to a new person—not necessarily a worse person or a better person, just a different person.

"I married you knowing you were getting a career started," the husband of a former high school teacher said. His wife's passionate and seemingly sudden desire to switch from professional educator to at-home mom threw him off balance because she had, until that point, all the appearances of "someone who was serious about a career."

"We had never consciously discussed this before marriage," says Leslie. "That's something I think is really important for people to do before they get married, at least to have that conversation and make sure you and your husband are both in line on that."

The fact that Leslie and her husband didn't have that conversation has made Leslie's experience a struggle.

That there is a struggle shouldn't be surprising. If you were a career woman who came home to raise your children, you're probably not doing the same things you had been doing for years. Instead of talking about the boss and wearing up-to-date clothes, jewelry, makeup (every day!), and confidence, you now may be chatting about the latest child development books and wearing sweats, spit-up stains, and uncertainty. You may have a new set of friends. You may face a new set of problems that your husband may not have the slightest idea how to help you solve. Your husband may feel as if he is walking on eggshells, wondering how to handle your transformation from progressive professional into maternal maven.

You might be confused about this radical shift in your lifestyle; isn't it logical that your husband might be a little disoriented as well?

# WHERE DO I FIT IN?

Because of the quantity of time a mother at home spends with her kids, she shares so many intimate secrets, plays so many games, makes so much history with her little one(s) that Dad may come home and feel like he's intruding on a private world. But you can help your husband by letting him know he is an essential component of that world. Moms and child-development experts alike know that babies and big kids need both parents to grow and develop into healthy, well adjusted children.

Dads and moms—working together but differently—are essential in providing the full scope of what a child needs to thrive physically and emotionally. For example, whereas mothers tend to provide peacefulness, fathers furnish playfulness; mom's touch is mostly tender, dad's touch is typically rough-and-tumble; mom's voice is most likely to be subdued and dad's voice is resounding. While mothers instill security and equity, fathers encourage independence and a competitive spirit. While mom's shouting "slow down!" to her daughter on the swing set, it's dad who's cheering, "go higher!" Sure, the differences may cause parenting disagreements at times, but the differences are healthy ones where the kids are concerned.

## DID YOU SAY WHAT I THINK YOU SAID?

In his efforts to pin down his role in your new stay-at-home mothering arrangement, your husband may be cueing in on mixed signals you're not meaning to send. For example, if you treat his homecoming each evening as an interruption in your day, he will feel like an interruption and perceptive kids will regard him that way too. But if you make him a special part of the daily routine, the time when he comes through the door each evening will be an anticipated time. Draw him into your days even when he's not there: Talk about him with the kids. Discuss what he's doing. Call or email him. Make special pictures and crafts for him to take to his office. Also, be sure to tell him some of the day's happy highlights when he gets home.

Another mixed message you may be giving your husband is saying you need help with the parenting but assigning him the dregs of parenting chores. "Annie's had a big day and now she's too cranky to settle down for sleep—here honey, you take her." "Would you

unload the dishwasher while I rock and feed the baby?"
These options give Dad a share of the duties all right,
but they don't give him a taste of the joys of having kids
in the house. So, since your husband does depend on
you to let him know how he can help, be sure to offer
a balanced list of "would-you's." Sure, you do need help
with Annie if she's cranky, especially after spending the
past 12 hours with her. Dad's touch might be just what
she needs for comfort. And you have indeed done
enough of the dirty work most days to deserve reaping
your rewards in the gaze of your little one's sleepy eyes
as she nestles in your arms to nurse. But make sure Dad
gets his fair share of the good stuff too!

# AM I OUT HERE IN THE RAT RACE, ALONE?

For possibly the first time in your married life, your
husband may be shouldering the full financial burden of
supporting your growing family. He may not be used to
the weight of this responsibility and its inherent pressures. Further, if you left the marketplace for at-home
motherhood, your husband may have lost with that exit
a mate who could identify and sympathize first-hand
with the problems of the workaday world. I was surprised how quickly I forgot about the minutiae of a
demanding career "out there": the incessant noise of
phones ringing; the presence of less-than-loving people;
the pressure of office politics; the stress of rush-hour

traffic jams; the weight of deadlines; the urgency of unmet quotas; the insistence of customers and clients; and the expectations of bosses. Your husband may feel he's lost his most empathetic partner. Train yourself to remember how the working world works. This will help you remind him that you're still his biggest supporter.

Here are some ideas to help keep colleague-type camaraderie alive even after you've scampered out of the rat race.

**Continue, at least occasionally, any business day routines you used to share.** If you used to meet for lunch each payday, arrange for a sitter once in a while so you can continue to enjoy that time together. If you rode into the city together, take him to work once in a while just to give him some company on the commute and jog your memory about the "pleasures" of Monday morning freeway traffic.

**Keep in touch with some of your former colleagues.** That will keep you up-to-date on the goings-on in your field. Your husband will likely enjoy hearing about the friends and the business he had become accustomed to hearing about before you quit.

**Ask your husband (and listen to the answers!) about his day at work,** his job, and the people he works with. Let him know you're still interested in his profession, although you've dropped out of yours.

**Commit yourself—body and soul—to his career.** Your new profession can become an asset to his. For example, Cyndi's husband, Shannon, serves as a full-time youth minister for a group of about 45 active teens. The former kindergarten teacher takes advantage of her time at home to give her husband a hand with time-consuming clerical chores, such as mailings, and to team up with him in planning special events.

"It's real exciting for me," Cyndi says. "It helps him to have another point of view, a female point of view, on things. I help him a lot." The added bonus, she says, is that "We get to spend a lot more time together ... he has hours he has to keep but it's okay for me to go with him."

As another example, Mike's job requires lots of entertaining. Since his wife, Tracy, used to work and didn't have much time to devote to housekeeping or hospitality, he had developed the habit of taking clients out for dinner. Now that she's home most of the time caring for their newborn son, she enjoys the chance to invite her husband's clients to their home. Mike loves the opportunity to share a bit of his home life with his clients, who relish the refreshing change from restaurant fare. Mike and Tracy (and their baby) all enjoy Mike's not having to be out as many evenings each month. Further, Tracy meets the people Mike talks about; putting faces to names makes his job even more interesting to her.

Commit yourself to becoming a prayer warrior for your husband, praying specifically and regularly that the Lord will guide him as he makes decisions, that the Lord will protect him—physically and spiritually—as he daily goes out into the world, that the Lord will bless his efforts to provide for your family, and that the Lord keeps him as the apple of His eye in the shadow of His wing (Psalm 17:8).

# LEFTOVERS ... AGAIN?

Mothering demands such presence of mind and such passion that you may find yourself emotionally and physically drained at the (working) day's end. You may not have much left over for your husband when he's home. Not only does this career require a hefty investment of heart and soul, but by nature it also dictates that your "bubble" of personal space (which, according to Psych 101, is crucial to one's emotional well-being) no longer exists. It drifted out the window and popped when the children came along. Infants, toddlers, and preschoolers alike enjoy nothing better than being within a six-inch perimeter of your body all day long.

It's sad, but not surprising, that when your husband comes home with outstretched arms at the end of the day, tired from work and longing for the love, affection, and attention of wife and kids, you make a mad dash in search of any room with a door that will lock to drink in what minutes of solitude you can sip before dinner. Your affection seems to have limits; you may feel like you simply don't have enough left over to be polite to the Fed Ex guy, much less to be warm and loving to your husband. It's critical to the health of your marriage to build into the day enough time and space to enable yourself to refuel your tank so you can be ready to return his affection without grimacing—because you need him as much as he needs you!

# On-the-Job Hazard!

## Becoming a Clinging Vine

While some days have you rushing into a private corner the moment your husband comes home, other days may find you greeting his homecoming with the desperate enthusiasm Gilligan's crew might have had upon spotting a rescue boat. You may feel like you've been stranded for the past eight hours on a remote island inhabited by demanding little natives. You're just dying to pour the details of adventures ("Corey's lizard got loose in the house today"); frustrations ("Bethany just isn't catching on to this potty thing"); and fears ("What if I choose the wrong preschool for Toby?" "What if we run out of diapers before I have the time to run to Wal-Mart?" "What if Shelby has picked up the stomach virus that's going around?") into an open ear.

But be careful not to let your sharing turn into nagging self-pity. No one wants to come home to that. It's good to let the pressure out of a boiling pot, and your husband may indeed hear you with a loving heart, sifting through the muck and mire of your day, keeping the gold and discarding the sand. However, avoid complete dependence on your husband as a lifeline to sanity and adulthood after a day in the trenches. He still has rough days at work too.

"At first, I depended on [my husband] for everything: conversation, recreation, home repairs, etc.," recalls one mom of her first weeks at home. She says she soon learned not to burden her husband with "every little detail of the day . . . [I] had to learn to make friends and get out with the kids without depending on him for every outing. He has his job and I have mine. Therefore, I don't gripe or complain about everything."

Another mom observes: "We love to wallow around as martyrs then yell at everybody for not fixing it. We expect so much from our husbands to fill so many needs in our lives, and we get so frustrated when they don't do this, that, or the other. God never intended for them to do [all of] this, that, or the other. Some of that stuff God's supposed to be doing. Some of that stuff we're supposed to be doing.

"So many women isolate themselves," she says. "They get holed up in their house with their children, they don't make any friends, and when their husbands get home, they yack their ears off and their husbands are just saying, 'I've been listening to people talk all day.' He just wants quiet; and then she's got her feelings hurt because he doesn't want to listen to her. She needs to find a friend to talk to during the day. She needs to invest herself in a friendship with another woman who also needs to talk so they can get that communication need met in a friendship instead of expecting their husbands to do that."

These wise moms must have been reading the quarrelsome wife passages in Proverbs:

It is better to
live in a corner of the
housetop than in a
house shared with a
quarrelsome wife.
(Proverbs 21:9)

It is better to live
in a desert land than
with a quarrelsome
and fretful woman.
(Proverbs 21:19)

A wife's quarreling is
a continual dripping of rain.
(Proverbs 19:13)

If you hold off bombarding him with that daily play-by-play and wait until he has had a chance to shed his tie and shake off any work-related problems that have followed him home, perhaps your husband will be ready to shift into the home mode to become the rescue boat you've been waiting for.

# WHEN DAD'S THE STAY-AT-HOME PARENT

Sometimes, for a variety of reasons, parents decide that it is dad, not mom, who stays at home with the kids. Mom may be bringing in a larger salary or better benefits than dad, so giving up his income seems more practical. Or it may be more feasible for a father to bring his career to a home office than for a mother. Professionally speaking, dad's career track may be the least disrupted by a parenting "time-out" than mom's; personally speaking, dad may simply feel led to stay at home while mom may sense God leading her to remain on the job.

Whatever the reason for the role reversal, the percentage of stay-at-home dads is on the rise. The number of children living with stay-at-home dads while mothers work has quadrupled since 1986 and is now the fastest-growing family type.

Males who choose this career track meet similar but perhaps more exaggerated challenges in their new roles. If stay-at-home moms are few and far between, consider how much harder it might be for stay-at-home dads to find a circle of colleagues to offer support and encouragement. The stay-at-home father culture, which is fairly new, seems to offer scant opportunities for men to combat isolation—one of the biggest issues resulting from that transition.

Despite the frustration involved in swimming against the current, dads can expect a hefty payoff for their efforts. Some of the benefits researchers say result from having dad at home full-time include higher grades, greater ambition, fewer anxiety disorders, expanded verbal skills, and a reduced risk of delinquency or teen pregnancy ("The Stay-at-Home Dad" by Suzanne Woods Fisher, *Christianity Today International/Marriage Partnership* [Fall 2000, Vol. 17, No. 3, 24] ).

A growing number of resources are working to equip fathers at home and help them make vital connections with one another. See Appendix C for a list.

# On-the-Job Hazard!

## Having a Tough Time Re-entering the Workforce

When a father has put his career on the back burner to take a parenting time-out, he may find his chances for re-entering the workforce have nearly boiled dry.

Potential employers don't always understand why a man would step off the career track for a season in order to care for his children. Stay-at-home fathers who want to get back to work once their kids have grown may find it tough to explain the gaps in the dates of the "work history" section of his résumé.

Career experts recommend that full-time dads and moms alike who would like to return to the work force maintain their job skills while they're off by volunteering or consulting and by staying on top of industry developments.

# Chapter 3

# your budget:
# money matters

> You shall have no other
> gods before Me. Exodus 20:3

In our society money is a god, and although money is not my god or yours, the economic demands of today's society often make it seem so when it becomes difficult, if not impossible, to make ends meet on just one salary.

"We drive old cars and wear the same clothes forever," says Amanda, mother of two, who's been at home for more than three years. Her comment echoes those of other at-home moms, many of whom say their decision to quit work has forced them to cut to the bare minimum financially. Inflation has jacked up basic living expenses—food, clothing, utilities, transportation, medical care, etc.—so the typical one-income family's lifestyle of today can't even begin to mirror the traditional one-earner family's two-story-house-in-the-suburbs lifestyle of previous decades. In addition, since society has in recent years redefined its meaning of "the average family" to denote "two-income family," what are considered *necessities* often encompass far more than families living on one income can afford. As a result, mother at home usually becomes synonymous with sacrifice as we struggle to stretch one-income finances around a two-income standard of living.

Among the prices some families say they've had to pay to have Mom stay at home: the chance to own a home, the security of having a savings account, the luxury of taking even modest vacations, the prospects of one or both parents finishing college, the benefit of participating in a company health insurance policy, and the opportunity for occasional dinner-and-movie nights out.

Parents of young children are a particular target of the marketplace and its ceaseless efforts to generate more revenues. Just walk through a mall and survey all the "kid gear" you see—nursery furniture, designer clothes and diapers, toys, CDs, exercise equipment, bottle warmers, traveling kits—all billed to new parents as *needs.* No one feels the pressure of that marketing more than we moms, who, because we always have our kids' best interests at heart, are by nature ever so vulnerable to becoming victims of the marketplace's winsome plays for our money. We find ourselves in the sometimes mentally exhausting routine of having to ask, *is this something I really need, or is this something society is telling me I need?*

Learning to distinguish needs from wants should be

top priority for families running a household on one income, says certified financial planner/investment broker Toney Brasuell, who writes a column about financial planning for a Christian magazine. Since his wife, Dawn, quit her job as a teacher to stay at home with their three children about 14 years ago, his family has experienced first-hand the budgeting challenges brought on when one parent leaves the marketplace. In his role as financial advisor, he has fielded many calls from couples asking for guidance as they make decisions about their newly slashed budget.

"I don't care whether it's $5,000 or $50,000 a year," Brasuell says, when a household income is reduced by any proportion, "there's still that hole in your budget it's going to leave."

He suggests couples work together to make a list to help them identify needs, giving careful thought to whether things like cell phones and cable television service are, in fact, necessities. "We did perfectly well without all that 20 years ago," he says. Once you have your list of needs, give it a second look to see if there's anything on it you can do without, "because you're most likely going to need to."

It's also important to scrutinize expenses related to insurance, Brasuell says, and to build a team of trustworthy providers you can count on to work with you to determine your best options.

"You need to make sure you're dealing with someone who's knowledgeable and whom you can trust to help you find out, once again, what's an absolute necessity and what's not."

For instance, Brasuell said one step he and his wife

took that made a dramatic difference in their insurance savings was to increase the deductible on their car insurance. "We did that 14 years ago and have not changed it since, and are not going to. You can save a considerable amount of money that way."

# HEAVENLY PROVISION

"I have learned in whatever situation I am to be content. I know how to be brought low, and I know how to abound. In any and every circumstance, I have learned the secret of facing plenty and hunger, abundance and need. I can do all things through Him who strengthens me" (Philippians 4:11–13).

Despite the often difficult adjustment involved in learning to make ends meet on the often humble means of one income, interviews with dozens of at-home moms didn't produce the whining cacophony of complaints I expected to hear as I delved into the sometimes annoying subject of finances. Rather, I found in the answers to my questions about dollars and cents a chorus of words similar to Paul's in the verses above—words telling of trust in God, faith in His promises, and contentment in less-than-ideal financial circumstances. Moms seem to be eager to share amazing tales of His provision, and agree that giving up the second income is a wonderful way to see just what God truly is capable of doing. Time and time again, stay-at-home moms relate powerful stories attesting to the hand of God on their lives following their decision to quit working outside the home.

"Every time when things get tight, I find another sacrifice I can make," said Tanya, who had been home with her daughter, Shelby, for three years before her son, Dalton, was born. "If we don't make the sacrifice, Shelby and Dalton will have to." Tanya, however, doesn't gripe about those sacrifices; instead, she cites to anyone willing to listen a testimonial laundry list of blessings she and her husband have been showered with since she left the workforce. For example, although they were on "just" one income—and with her husband attending college full-time to boot—when she first quit work, the couple was able to purchase a home and a car.

As Tanya's and many other families' stories illustrate, "my God will supply every need of yours according to His riches in glory in Christ Jesus" (Philippians 4:19).

However, He also expects us to make use of the gift of common sense and do our best with what He has supplied. See the story of the wise steward in Luke 19:11–27. The lesson is clear: If we seek spiritual gain in the Gospel, for ourselves and others (including our husbands and children), we will become richer. If we neglect or squander what we have been given, we will become impoverished, losing even what we have. Note that "richer" doesn't mean if we put God first we'll be financially set for life. It means that we will be under the care of a loving God, who has promised to provide for our needs even as He provides for the smallest sparrow.

It's not about the riches of this world, after all; it's about the riches of the kingdom of God.

"I will give up every material possession I own because I know that I can't get to heaven pulling my little red wagon full of all my things," stay-at-home mom Diana Ferrell told a group of mothers when she was speaking at a women's event at her church. "But with the grace of God I can get there along with my children."

# STRONG BUDGET STRATEGIES

God knows we're human. He knows how easy it can be to make mistakes that will bury us in financial difficulty. So He gives us many wonderful resources to help us develop good money management principles and plan our budgets. Check your local bookstore or library for resources offering solid, sensible budgeting advice or sign up for that class on Christian stewardship at your church. And consider following the tips below for making it easier to make ends meet.

## 1. Just Say No

Saying no might be the first course offered in stay-at-home mom's basic budget training, if there were such a thing. "No, I can't subscribe to your magazine (no matter how good it is)," I've told many a salesperson over the phone. "I'm sorry, I don't think I'll be able to join you," I have had to tell friends proposing lunch outings. "I'll have to stick to the package," I have staunchly stated while a photography studio salesperson displayed eight-by-tens of my rosy-cheeked and beribboned 4-month-old that I would do anything (besides bounce a check) to take home and hang over the fireplace. "Why are the photos that come in the advertised specials never as good as the ones we have

# On-the-Job Hazard!

**Losing Control of the Purse Strings**

"Honey, can I have some money?" This can be an uncomfortable question for a woman to ask her husband. As women who are brought up in a society that fosters independence and self-sufficiency, giving up our income not only strains the family budget, it can sever our sense of self-sufficiency in the area of family finances.

"Losing the control that comes with earning a paycheck is the hardest part" of going to a one-income lifestyle, says Dawn, who's been at home for 13 years. "It is harder to manage money I did not earn than money I did earn."

The answer? Unfortunately, there's not an easy one. But possibly the single most important thing we can do is to have a series of money talks with our mates. Talk about your budget and how you'll divide spending responsibilities. Discuss how much regular income you need to cover household expenses, child rearing, and pocket money day in and day out. Evaluate whether separate checking accounts might be practical and decide who will be in charge of paying what bills. The more arrangements you discuss and put into place, the less your chances of financial flare-ups.

to pay extra for?" I've moaned, watching the person across the table gather up and file away the poses our two-digit checking account balance simply wouldn't cover.

The list goes on. You may have to say no instead of scraping up the cash for a one-day-a-week Mother's

Day Out program, although it would give you a much-needed break. "No" might be your response to a friend's suggestion that you keep your post-maternity self-esteem—as well as your midsection—from drooping by signing up for mom-and-tot exercise classes at the local fitness club. You might even have to say no to a picnic in the park if you don't have enough cash on hand to put gas in the tank to get you there. The trick is, if we learn to say no with grace to the well-intended invitations and offers that we deem desirable but not affordable, we learn to savor even more heartily the times our budgets allow us to say yes.

## 2. Cut Corners

Saying no may be one of the most effective methods of budget control, but it's not always an option. You still have to eat, wear clothes, heat your home, get haircuts, buy gifts . . . the list goes on and on. Since mothers at home seem to have cornered the market on cutting corners, take a look at a few of the following penny-pinching and budget-stretching ideas they've shared to see if some of their tips might work for you.

Many moms at home learn to save lots of money by shopping garage sales, estate sales, and resale shops. Some hints for the used-goods markets? Carefully inspect clothing before buying. Fifty cents for a sweater is 50¢ too much if the sweater has a stain or a hole. Best clothing buys at these sales are:

**INFANT WEAR**—Because infants outgrow clothing so quickly, they don't play outside in the mud, and don't wear out the knees crawling around. Watch for milk stains on collars, though.

**OUTERWEAR/PLAYWEAR**—I once paid $3 for a size 3T, warmly lined winter coat. I bought it for Nick, then 2, to wear when he played outside in the sandbox and in the occasional snow Arkansas winters provide. It fit him for two winters, then Lindsey wore it for messy outdoor play. Having that coat saved wear and tear on their good coats. The same goes for jeans and other durable play clothes. Buy seconds for the kids to play in and save their new clothes for birthday parties, play group, and church.

**SPECIAL OCCASION**—Easter dresses and suits, Christmas clothes, etc. This is a big money saver because this kind of clothing usually goes virtually unworn.

**TOYS**—Besides clothing, watch second-hand outlets for toys in good shape. Buying used toys often allows us room to buy more: Why buy a new set of Legos for $15 at the super center when you can pick up a tub of them, a game, and some dress-up clothes for $7 at a yard sale?

In addition to haunting yard sales and resale shops, most stay-at-home moms say they watch sale papers, clip coupons, buy generic-brand products, buy in large quantities (especially on-sale products), and carefully consider each purchase to stretch the budget from one paycheck to the next.

Other ways moms adapt lifestyles to suit a one-income budget include:

**Planting a garden**—Even a few peppers, tomatoes, and herbs planted each summer can help you save bucks on the makings for great salsa, dips, salads, and garnishes.

**Using cloth diapers**—I did this for one of my children when we were at home and saved disposables for when we went out. It's really not as bad as you might think—give it a try!

**Hanging clothes out on the line to dry.**

**Learning to sew.**

**Learning a craft to make gifts.**

**Always using the dishwasher's air dry setting.**

**Getting simple hairstyles** that don't need to be cut as often.

**Going home from the beauty salon wet** (getting a cut instead of a cut and style).

**Watching the thermostat setting** and eliminating unnecessary use of lights.

**Recycling and cash-for-trash programs.**

**Holding annual or semi-annual garage sales.**

**Sharing videos and magazines** with other families.

**Driving used (paid for) cars.**

**Taking good quality used clothing and household goods to a resale shop.**

**Cooking from scratch** more often to avoid buying expensive prepared foods.

**Fixing your husband a brown-bag lunch.**

**Paying off bills and stashing the credit cards.** To

pay off their bills, one mother of three who's been home for more than five years says she and her husband "snowball" bills by paying off one bill, then putting the money they had been accustomed to spending on that bill toward the next bill on their list, and so on. After all the bills are paid off, a good motto to adopt is "if you don't have cash, you can't afford it," says another mom.

**Buying on credit seldom, if ever**—"If you have to borrow money for something, allow yourself only one debt at a time," suggests Theresa, a mother of two who's been at home for two years.

## 3. Do It Yourself

Moms are renowned for creativity, which comes in handy when it comes to living on a budget. If you can make your own clothes, cut your kids' hair, color/perm your own hair, make artsy-craftsy gifts to sock away for Christmas and birthdays, design your own birthday party decorations, garden, can, and make bows for gift wrap and for your little girls' ponytails, you'll be able to trim a good deal off expenses. Further, if you and your husband, as a team, can tackle household repairs and re-dos yourselves rather than hiring help, you'll save even more money.

Along these lines, exchanging favors is another good money stretcher. For example, if I arrange flowers and my friend sews, I might do the flowers for a shower she's giving and she, in return, might hem my new dress. For another friend, I might address in calligraphy some invitations to a fundraiser she's planning; she might help me wallpaper my bathroom in return.

For most mothers at home (especially those without family nearby), baby-sitting is a hot commodity. Try trading kids with another mom for a free mother's day out every other week. Couples can swap kids every other Friday night for a night out (or in!). Or try starting a baby-sitting co-op like the one Shannon, mother of two, is involved in. Take note! This is a gem, if you can round up enough committed participants. "Twenty families participate," explains Shannon. "We each get 20 cards, each card representing one hour of baby-sitting for one child. Instead of hiring a baby-sitter, we call on one another to help take care of kids and we pay one card per hour per child. If I baby-sit, I get cards too . . . so it's an even trade."

## 4. Stretch Your Entertainment Dollars

Keeping household expenses within the budget can be simple enough to do from Monday through Friday, but with each TGIF comes that let's-get-out-of-the-house feeling that can quickly turn into a budget-buster.

One night during our first year of marriage, when money was especially tight, Kurt and I got home from work and really wanted to go out and eat. I mean, we really wanted to go out and grab a pizza. We were tired and hungry, and nothing in the refrigerator or the pantry sounded good. So we headed to the bedroom to change out of our work clothes, discussing all the while how we could rationalize spending the money. When Kurt slipped his hand into his jeans pocket, he was surprised to pull out a crumpled $10 bill. There was our answer! Without any more discussion about the matter, we grabbed our jackets and headed out the door.

I really believed at the time—and still do—that God knew how important it was for young and struggling newlyweds to get out and do some of the things they used to do before the realities of marriage and running a household kicked in. That was His way of shooing us out the door and telling us to have fun. To this day, I sense God's blessing on the times Kurt and I make time for dates with each other—as well as when we treat the whole family to a special dinner out.

Because getting out of the house together and doing things both as a family and as a couple is so important, one-income families can find ways to do so without blowing the bank account. Figure a certain amount into the budget so you can enjoy guilt-free excursions on those weekend nights when the sun is setting and you're feeling like being anywhere but home, and on those Saturday afternoons when the desire to see at least one movie at a real theater (as opposed to waiting a year for the video to be released) overtakes you.

For some low-cost or free fun, check out the following ideas:

**PICNICS**

**CAMPING**

**"KIDS EAT FREE" NIGHTS** at restaurants

**COMMUNITY FESTIVALS,** such as holiday fireworks shows

**LIBRARIES**—Check with yours for a listing of programs offered. Some offer film festivals, etc.

**TAKE A DRIVE**—possible romantic destinations include a sunset drive downtown (I love to catch the sight of a bride and groom ducking into a limo outside the lobby of a nice hotel), in the country, or along the nearest river or lake. One mom says she and her family like to drive around and play "Slug Bug" (remember the spot-the-Volkswagen Beetle game we played when we were kids?)

**COLLEGES AND UNIVERSITIES,** churches, and civic organizations often sponsor free or low-cost plays and musical productions. Holiday productions are an especially nice option during a time when the budget is stretched even tighter.

**ZOO**—Usually not too expensive; watch for admission specials or coupons, and pack a picnic to avoid paying high prices for concessions.

**DOLLAR THEATER** or matinee showings at regular-priced theater.

**HIGH SCHOOL AND JUNIOR HIGH SPORTING EVENTS** (could be especially romantic if you married your high-school sweetheart and you still live in the same town).

**DROP BY FRIENDS' HOUSE** (call first!) or invite them to yours. It doesn't always have to be for dinner. We've been through times when we received so many dinner invitations that we felt obliged not to invite friends over unless it was to eat with us. That's great sometimes, but it's also fun (and less expensive) to ask them to drop by after dinner for a game of cards or a rented movie. Pop some popcorn and enjoy the fellowship. If you do want to extend a

dinner invitation, however, cut costs by choosing a simple, inexpensive meal and splurging on a special dessert (picking up a gallon of that name-brand ice cream you rarely buy). Pick some flowers from the yard or put a bowl of fresh fruit on the table for a centerpiece and light some candles, and you'll have an elegant meal to share. If you're in the mood for a dinner party, tell your guests you'll provide the salad, baked potatoes, corn on the cob, and dessert, and let them each bring their favorite meat to throw on the grill.

**MALL**—People-watching and window-shopping can be fun ways to pass a couple of hours at the mall. Kurt and I love to browse bookstores and music stores. (Beware! The fun isn't fun anymore when the sight of all the new things you can't buy depresses you, or worse, tempts you to the point that you give in and spend money you shouldn't.)

For more great tips on saving money, do a cyber-search using the key word "frugal." You will be surprised how many great Web sites there are that are loaded with of penny-pinching tactics.

# On-the-Job Hazard!

## Wanting it All

I'm going to open up a very private area of my heart to you because I think it's important to acknowledge one particular threat that endangers the contentment of a woman who's mothering at home. Although God and my hard-working husband have always provided me and our family with every-thing we have needed and much of what we have wanted, for many years I struggled against envy—which I realize now was also tangled up with pride. I wanted to be at home, but I didn't like having to live there on a one-income lifestyle—clipping coupons, wearing outdated clothes, and driving older vehicles. I wanted to raise my own children day in and day out, but I also wanted to be able to take them to Chuck E. Cheese whenever I liked; to dress them in cute, trendy styles; and to treat the teacher to lunch.

Interestingly, the issue of wanting to have as much as others around me seldom surfaced during my first few years at home. I guess it's because during those first years, many of our friends were also starting out in their marriages and careers; none of us had that much, materially speaking, any-way. With a few exceptions, our houses were of similar size and age, our vacations were equally moderate or nonexistent, and we shopped at the same discount stores. It wasn't until our two-income counterparts got a few years of working and saving under their belts that I began to see the distinction between our spending habits and lifestyles increasing at lightning speed. While they were moving up to live in bigger and better homes, spending from more comfortably padded checkbooks, and shopping at more upscale stores, we seemed to be standing still. We were living in the same house, which seemed smaller and older each year. We were still writing checks on a limited spending account, and we continued to shop at resale shops and discount centers. Try as I might, I didn't feel content standing materially still.

Be assured, in my heart I knew that people, not things, mattered. I was doing what I believed God had told me to do and trusted that He would provide for us. My emotions, however, were pulling out all stops to persuade me otherwise. I was hearing whispered lies like these:

"If I were a better Christian, God would be showering us with more material blessings."

"Maybe my kids would be better off if I go back to work so we could afford extras they're having to do without."

"I deserve a _____ more than she does since I do _____ and she doesn't."

Pretty ugly attitude, isn't it?

Finally, not willing to be content with feeling so discontent all the time, I embarked on a treasure hunt in the Bible. I determined to spend my quiet time each day roaming through the concordance to find answers to my questions about how to deal with envy and desire. Just as God promises, when I asked, He began to answer my questions day by day as I sprawled across my bed looking up verse after verse. My heart was humbled by warnings about the destructive nature of envy. My vision of the eternal benefits of staying home to raise my kids was brought into clearer focus by reminders that temporal things are just that: temporary. And my emotions—the things that had caused me so much heart trouble to begin with—were delighted when I learned that the desire of God's heart is to give me the desires of my heart . . . when I trust Him completely.

If, you are like me and envy—or for that matter any other destructive emotion or behavior—is hampering your ability to celebrate your life as a stay-at-home mom, I challenge you to open your Bible and launch a similar search. You'll be glad you did. To help you get started, see Appendix D in the back of the book for some key topics and verses.

## 5. Earn Some Extra Money

They are to teach what is good, and so train the young women . . . to be self-controlled, pure, working at home. (Titus 2:4–5)

Nowhere is it written that parents who want to raise their own kids must divorce themselves from anything having to do with commerce. Whether you work for others—via telecommuting, flextiming or moonlighting—or for yourself, moms and dads at home find all kinds of ways to drum up income ranging from a full salary with benefits to a little bit of mad money. Some take their professional careers home either full time or part time. One woman who ran the in-house advertising office for a large food distributor was able to continue some of her responsibilities part time after her baby came by editing and publishing the company newsletter on a personal computer at home. Another woman who had worked as a floral designer for years brought her expertise home as a part-time wedding consultant. Her work took her away from the kids only on weekends, when her husband could take over.

In addition, many professionals continue their work on a freelance or consulting basis.

If your career isn't that portable—that is, it doesn't lend itself to being taken home—this could be just the time to turn a hobby into a business, sharpen a marketable skill, or start a completely new career. Investigate selling products for Avon, Tupperware, Pampered Chef, or other similar types of companies to see if that would be right for you. Hit the road with your handmade quilts by plugging into the arts and crafts fair circuit. Paint signs, cut hair, desktop publish, design web pages, baby-sit, run errands, do bookkeeping, clean homes, plan parties, cater parties, upholster furniture, letter invitations in calligraphy, or do any of dozens of other tasks.

If starting a home business interests you, it's important to do your research. Start by reading books, checking with the Small Business Administration's Small Business Development Center, and asking advice from others you know who are making working at home work. If you don't have an entrepreneurial spirit, starting up a new business may not suit you. Take a serious look at your energy level, drive, and family support. The Lord gives us all different gifts; not everyone is equipped to run a home-based business.

If working at home isn't for you, part-time or temporary work might be. Tonya, mother of three, is a registered nurse who works weekends for a home-health agency. Because she lives near the hospital and the patients she's assigned to see, she can even dash home for an hour or two at a stretch in between visits, giving her ample time to nurse her newborn son, throw a load of laundry in the washing machine, shuttle her 4-year-old daughter to a birthday party, or catch the final innings of her oldest son's ball game.

Another woman took a Tuesday/Thursday job in a pediatrician's office after her daughter turned 2 and was ready for the social interaction a neighborhood child-care center offered. Another mom found her ideal situation by working as a temp, filling in a week here and a few days there for vacationing employees at the company where she worked before the kids came along. And yet another works as a substitute teacher, taking on as many days a month as she wants or needs to supplement the family budget. "Being a substitute teacher helps me maintain my skills and still be at home most of the time," says Patty, mother of one and stepmother of two.

How might you go about finding such family-friendly work situations?

**Network. Let everyone you know what your skills or interests are,** and let them know you're looking for part-time work. Most people in the working world assume you're at home to take care of the kids—which you are. But they (probably) won't assume you'd like them to throw some income opportunity your way unless you tell them.

**Stay in touch with former employers and coworkers.** Sometimes they find it hard to replace you, and after you've been gone a while they would gladly hand over some work. They may also let you know about job openings and management changes that could bring about new opportunities.

**Read the classifieds in the local paper.** You just never know what you'll stumble into. (I told you what happened to me in Chapter 1!)

**Read periodicals and newsletters in your field of interest.** This will keep fresh ideas rolling in, help you keep up with what's new and what's news in your area, and may give you some job-winning leads to pursue.

Working at home, telecommuting, working part-time, or temporary work may not pan out for you. For example, the money may not be as good as you hoped — after you subtract such expenses as gas, business equipment and supplies, clothes, child care, or the fast-food dinners you may be buying because you don't have time to cook. And your new home business may do so well you find you are working as much or more than you were when you worked outside the home, possibly defeating your goal of improved quality of family life. Although your hours may be flexible and you may be your own boss, it's inevitable that when you work with or for others you (at times) have to accommodate their needs—even when it doesn't fit into your family's schedule. The way I get my work-at-home work done is by heading for the computer many evenings as soon as Kurt comes in the door. He takes over with the kids and in the kitchen. So I miss out on some family time, and it is a sacrifice. It's important to think about these issues before you make any decisions. And pray diligently, asking your heavenly Father for wisdom and discernment as you take each step.

Whatever you decide, know this: nothing is permanent. Any work arrangement you make can be changed to fit your and your family's needs. As you take full advantage of God's gift of common sense to work through your work arrangements, remember that He is faithful to you. The anxiety of budget challenges is relieved by relying on God's Word.

# your job site: gearing up for growing kids

> She looks well to the ways of her household.
> Proverbs 31:27

It doesn't take most of us long to learn that our job descriptions entail more than the routine care and feeding of our children. Amid the bathing, feeding, bottle giving, diapering, lunch cooking, hand washing, potty training, and naptimes, we must strategically insert play dough sessions, story times, playground jaunts, songs, games, and other learning activities. Otherwise, our little customers aren't getting their money's worth.

But finding ways to keep our children safe, healthy, and out of the whiny clutches of boredom isn't easy, especially considering we have homes to run in the meantime. So we have to muster all the creativity and energy we have to best fill the hours each Tuesday, Friday, Sunday, Thursday, Saturday, Monday, and Wednesday that God hands us.

Remember that imaginary first-day-on-the-job scenario in Chapter 1? Well, imagine that instead of showing you an empty office to furnish and arrange in a way to most efficiently suit your needs, your new boss opens the front door of your home, saying, "Here's your new office." It's up to you to design your "workplace," where you'll be caring for and nurturing healthy, happy children for the next season of life you'll be sharing.

## TOOLS OF THE TRADE

The most elegant offices don't do their employees much good unless desks are topped with phones and computers, supply closets are full of paper and pens, and file cabinets are loaded with files. Likewise, homes that look like they belong in the latest issue of *Better Homes & Gardens* don't do their resident kids much good unless the closets, cabinets, shelves, and storage chests are fully stocked with the tools of the trade. Thumb through the following catalog of some of the supplies in a well-equipped home.

## TOYS

Toys may seem like child's play to just any old

grown-up, but moms, dads, and other child development and education professionals know otherwise. The importance of toys in the life of a household with kids takes on an even greater proportion for moms at home. Children who spend their days in childcare situations away from home have the advantage of access to two different sets of toys. By the time they've begun to lose interest in the offering of toys presented at their day-care center, baby-sitter's, or grandma's house, evening rolls around, reuniting them with their own set of familiar standbys. Kids at home, however, can easily tire of their toys if we don't take seriously the fun job of gathering them.

## CHOOSY MOTHERS CHOOSE . . .

We've all, at one time or another, been taken for a ride by toys that either lost our child's interest after a half-hour session or broke after five minutes of play. When selecting toys to buy, borrow, or beg from eager-to-please grandparents, follow these guidelines:

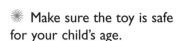 Make sure the toy is safe for your child's age.

✳ Make sure the toy is appropriate for your child's developmental stage.

✳ Make sure the toy is fun and stimulating.

✳ Make sure the toy and what it represents fits your system of values.

✳ Make sure 90 percent of the play relies on the child and 10 percent on the toy.

When scouting for toys, don't be a toy snob, choosing only those that are brand new and name brand. Store-bought, homemade, or rescued from the attic, a high-quality toy can be anything your child likes to play with, whether it's a cardboard box, a wooden spoon, a cowbell picked up at a flea market, or a bucket of seashells gathered during last summer's vacation. To stretch a toy's playing time, mix and match. When your little tyke is playing with cars, get out the blocks to make some buildings for the cars to drive around and through. If he's playing with tractors, get a box lid filled with popcorn kernels, dry beans, or uncooked rice and let him plow through the "turf." When your little one is playing with the doctor's kit, rustle up stuffed animal patients and a uniform from the dress-up bin. For a tea party, get out the crayons and paper and let your child design the invitations. The combinations are endless; be creative!

Browse through the following toy section of our catalog as if you were strolling down the aisle of a toy store. You may already have many of these items, and most don't represent much of a financial investment if you don't. Keep in mind age appropriateness. This list comes from a variety of sources, including other stay-at-home moms, my own experience, and the books *Early Education at Home* by M. Jean Soyke and *How to Parent* by Fitzhugh Dodson.

# TOYS, TOYS, AND MORE TOYS

**BAGS, BACKPACKS, AND PURSES**—kids need things to put their collections of other things in.

**BALLOONS**—talk about cheap thrills; see page 114 for a few fun balloon play ideas.

**BALLS**—of all sizes to roll, throw, bounce, toss, hide, sit on, balance on one's head . . .

**BLANKETS**—okay, this isn't really a toy. But when my children were toddlers, I would have shuddered at the thought of spending even one day without a couple of blankets to eat snacks on in front of the TV, to swaddle dolls and stuffed animals, to pull kids around on, to clothespin around necks for super-hero capes, to wrap around heads for would-be shepherds, to make tents out of, to designate play areas—("You play with these blocks on your blanket, and you play with these on yours") . . .

**BLOCKS**—plain wooden blocks are great. So are dominoes and empty boxes (shoe, cereal, etc.) stuffed with newspaper or tissue, then taped shut. And so are interlocking blocks: Lego, Duplo, Waffle, Bristle, etc.

**BOXES**—big ones, as in refrigerator or television. Snatch them up whenever you can. Refrigerator boxes can become forts, boats, or castles, and television-sized boxes make good cars. When the boxes start falling apart, cut them up into good-sized boards to sit on to slide down the nearest grassy or snowy hill or to prop against the swing set or a tree for yet another hideout. Save even smaller boxes such as shoe, shirt, or jewelry boxes, too. Use them to make doll and stuffed animal furniture, buildings, cars, trains, and treasure chests. For instance, round oatmeal or cornmeal boxes offer endless possibilities.

**CARDS**—the playing kind. Good for games of concentration, matching, sorting, and building houses.

**TOY CARS, PLANES, AND TRAINS**—You don't have to spend a fortune on all the trimmings. Draw a customized roadway or city for the vehicles with a permanent marker or paint pen on a cheap vinyl tablecloth.

**CONSTRUCTION TOYS**—Lego, Duplo, Zak, clothespins, Tinkertoys, Lincoln Logs, Erector sets, toolbench sets. Styrofoam packing forms make good accompaniments to tool bench sets; little ones can easily drive in plastic nails with their lightweight hammers.

**DIRT**—The cheapest item on the list! Stocked with sticks, plastic dishes, spoons, and a water source, this is the spot that kids' dreams are made of.

**DOCTOR'S KIT**—embellish with some real medical supplies: bandages, tweezers, an empty, cleaned antiseptic bottle and cotton balls, a memo pad and pencil for prescriptions, etc. Lay a sheet of white wrapping tissue on your child's table so she can lay her animal and doll friends on the table to take care of them, just like her doctor does.

**DOLLS AND STUFFED ANIMALS**—companions, patients, customers, babies, sisters, brothers, stu-

dents, pets—dolls and stuffed animals become all
these things and more to kids.

**DRESS-UP CLOTHES**—Look (on clearance
racks, at garage sales, at estate sales, through hand-
me-downs) for such dress-up-chest treasures as hats,
gloves, scarves, athletic uniforms, military uniforms,
cheerleading uniforms, fancy gowns, vests, coats, jackets, shoes, purses, ties, wallets, briefcases, belts,
watches, necklaces, bracelets, etc. Include in your col-
lection aluminum foil (make crowns and shields) and
chenille sticks (twist onto headbands for antennae).
Most important, keep a full-length mirror—and your
camera—nearby!

**JUNK MAIL**—recycling at its best. From junk mail,
kids can glean "real" credit cards, stickers (especially
from those magazine-peddling packages), pictures to
cut out and make puzzles from, envelopes to fill up,
forms to fill out, and scrap paper to make planes
from or to wad up into artillery for a paper war.
Keep a stack of it by the phone, where you most
often need a quick distraction to hand over in
exchange for a few moments of undisturbed conversation.

**MAKEUP**—save cosmetic-drawer empties (if they're
kid-safe) and put them in a makeup bag with some
cotton balls, cotton-tipped swabs, old makeup brushes and sponges, and a plastic bottle or two of water
for some mess-free makeup fun.

**MARBLES**—great with toilet and paper towel tubes
masking-taped together to make chutes. Help your
children create games by taping multiple chutes inside
cardboard boxes.

**MUSICAL TOYS**—whether they're the made-for-kids kind, the made-for-grown-ups kind (picked up for a few dollars at a garage sale), or the homemade-from-paper-towel-tubes-and-tissue-and-combs kind, they're all real to kids who need to make some music.

**OUTSIDE TOYS**—bikes, trikes, balance beams, swings, tires, monkey bars, slides, wagons, balls, shovels, rakes, kites, etc.

**PAPER DOLLS**—dime-store-bought or, better yet, homemade by cutting out a simple doll shape and kid-designed clothes that can be attached with paper clips or bobby pins. To make the doll sturdy for repeated use, "laminate" it with clear contact paper.

**PEOPLE**—little plastic ones. And animal figurines too. To play with in dollhouses, block houses, pretend cities, play farms, etc.

**PUPPETS**—Purchased ones are great; homemade are better. Look through the arts and crafts basket for ideas, then stage a rendition of your little ones' favorite storybook or Bible story.

**PUZZLES**—store-bought or homemade: glue colorful magazine pictures onto cardboard; cut into puzzles as difficult or as easy as your child enjoys.

**ROPE**—My folks took Nick to the lake for the weekend and reported that he played with a rope for two solid hours. What he did with it, I'm not sure. But I felt that two hours' worth of entertainment value makes any toy, no matter how humble, worthy of this list.

**SAND**—See "dirt," above, only sand's not quite as messy and you can build things with it. Invest in fancy sandbox toys or round up old strainers and sifters from the kitchen. Another easy idea: staple some scraps of screen to the backs of smooth wooden frames for your little gold diggers (picture frames from the dollar store are great for this).

**STRING AND BEADS** or buttons, or even macaroni or tube pasta.

**AUDIOCASSETTE** player and tapes.

# TOY TIP:
## STORAGE & RETRIEVAL

Glancing through cute kids' room spreads in glossy parenting magazines or on home decorating shows often leaves us wondering why the kids using those rooms don't have many toys. Often, all we see is an intelligently placed globe or an artistically propped baseball bat and glove. In real life, however, we stuff toys into closets, we stack them on shelves. We cram them under beds, we hang them from hooks. We stash them in nets, we store them in containers ranging from designer-colored stacking bins and wicker baskets to rinsed-out potato-chip cans and empty baby-wipe boxes. We scoot the biggest and bulkiest toys (race tracks, dollhouses, etc.) against the wall where we soon begin to consider them part of our decorating scheme.

"So where can I store all these toys and playthings?" you ask. Regardless of whether you use shelves, toy boxes, milk crates, or paper sacks, follow these two simple rules: (1) pick a place for each toy and let that be its home and, (2) make every effort to keep all the toys and their respective parts and parts of parts intact.

Allowing children ready access to their most-loved toys makes your job a lot easier: You don't have to spend time and footsteps fetching this and getting that. However, there's also something to be said for denying access to certain possessions. Most of the moms I've talked with keep at least some of their kids' toys out of reach to keep them fresh and fun. In our house, dime store trinkets and toy store extravagances are equally special if they are stored on a high shelf that only grown-ups can reach.

Some moms design inventory control systems with extraordinary finesse. "Just before Christmas," says one mother of three, "I pack away two big boxes of toys to make room for the new toys the kids will be getting." Then, she says, sometime around July, when her girls are good and tired of the dolls, blocks, and puzzles that dazzled them at Christmas, she pulls out those boxes of forgotten friends. Happily reunited with their old gizmos and gadgets, her girls are good to go for the home stretch before another holiday season rolls around. Note: When you pack toys for storage, be sure to remove the batteries. Also keep in mind whether the toys might be damaged by moisture or excessive heat if you're storing them in a damp basement or an un-air-conditioned attic or storage shed.

Another mom says her daughter's birthday is so close to Christmas that she and her husband buy toys for these occasions that are "a little hard to play with" so their daughter can grow into them later in the year as she outgrows and becomes bored with her simpler toys.

# Arts and Crafts Supplies

Now we come to the arts and crafts section of our catalog. For ideas on how to stock your arts and crafts shelf, basket, box, or bag, take cues from the supply room of your church's preschool department. You'll probably find the following:

**BRADS**

**CARDBOARD**

**CHALK**

**CLOTHESPINS**

**CONTACT PAPER**—clear, for certain crafts and for preserving special drawings.

**COTTON BALLS**

**CRAYONS**

**CREPE PAPER**

**GLITTER**

**GLUE**

**MARKING PENS**—washable, unless you enjoy living on the edge.

**PAINT**—watercolor, finger, and poster (Note: For homemade finger paint, mix flour, salt, and food color to the desired consistency and shade.)

**PAPER**—tissue paper (colored and white), lined notebook paper, construction paper, and inexpensive drawing paper—lots of it. Check with your local newspaper as a possible source. Ours sells clean end-rolls of newsprint for 50¢ per pound. I bought one heavier than I could carry alone when Nick was 3 and it doodled him all the way into first grade.

**PAPER CLIPS**

**PASTE**

**PENCILS**

**PENCIL SHARPENER**

**PLASTIC MESH**

**PLAY DOUGH**—Sure, you can buy it, and it's not all that expensive, but it's really easy and fun to make: Stir together 1 cup flour, 1/2 cup salt, 1 cup water, 1 teaspoon cream of tartar, 1 tablespoon oil, and a few drops of food coloring. Cook over medium heat, stirring until well blended. When mixture begins to pull together, remove from heat and cool until you and the kids can knead it until it's smooth. Then it's ready to roll. Store in an airtight container in the fridge; it will last for several weeks.

**CRAFT STICKS**—to build with or spread paste with

**COTTON SWABS**

**RIBBON SCRAPS**

**RUBBER BANDS**

**RULER**

**SCISSORS**

**SPONGES**

**STENCILS**

**STRAWS**

**STRING**

**TAPE**—masking and cellophane

**TOOTHPICKS**

**YARN**

In no other area is being a junkaholic so politically correct. So, since one mother's trash is often a bored child's treasure, here's a list of "junk" you might want to think twice about before tossing. These make for great craft-time supplies.

**BERRY CONTAINERS**

**BOXES**

**BUTTER TUBS**

**BUTTONS**—before you relegate old clothing to the rag bin, snip off the buttons (and zippers) for the scrap box.

**CATALOGS**

**EGG CARTONS**

**FABRIC SCRAPS**

**GREETING CARDS** (used)

**JUNK MAIL**

**LIDS**—from milk cartons or aerosol cans.

**MAGAZINES**

**PAPER SACKS** (all sizes)

**SAWDUST**—Makes great clay: Mix one part flour to two parts sawdust, add water until the concoction sticks together. Let the projects dry for a day or two, then sand and paint the particle-board-like creations.

**SOCKS**

**TUBES**—from paper towels, toilet paper, wrapping paper, aluminum foil, and plastic wrap.

# BOOKS

The benefits of nurturing a love of books and reading are no secret. Children who are read to have an easier time learning to read, develop longer attention spans, and cultivate worldviews often broader than those of kids who haven't been exposed to literature.

But the value of introducing children to books at an early age extends far past merely improving a child's chances for academic success. Simply taking the time to read to your children shows them that books are important to you. In the Christian home, books take on an even greater significance: They can become adventure-filled paths along which family relationships can be strengthened, values and morals instilled, and sensitive subjects approached and discussed, all within the sphere of Bible-based reading. Most important, nurturing a love of books and reading in young children can help Christian parents lay the groundwork for teaching the faith and developing a love of the most important story of all in the most important book of all—the Bible.

Take as much, if not more, care in selecting books as when selecting toys. Naturally, consider the age and reading level of the book. Also give serious thought to whether the story will interest your kids. It's important that you look over each book first to make sure its message and artwork fit within the framework of what you consider morally acceptable. For instance, evolutionism runs rampant among children's literature, as do refrains of New Age, humanistic philosophies, and muddied doctrine. Read the books before you buy them.

You don't have to spend much money to build a great children's library. I've got what I consider to be a pretty good one—without subscribing to pricey book clubs or blowing my grocery money at the mall bookstore. Many people unload great titles at garage sales and second-hand shops. If a book's in great condition, I'm thrilled; but if it's a little worn, I don't really mind. I like to think about another mother in another home reading the same words to her own little ones.

# ELECTRONICS

TV/VCR/DVD players, video games, and computers in a household are double-edged swords with which parents can skillfully battle their kids' boredom. On the one hand, using the tube can get out of hand. Thirty-minute, back-to-back cartoon or sitcom reruns can melt into hours if you don't use the off button and put the remote out of reach. The luster of favorite movies on VHS or DVD fade when we let kids watch these flicks over and over. And children may become consumed with the desire to play "just one more level" if we don't set limits on the entertainment systems and computer.

However, the majority of moms I surveyed and interviewed do use the TV/VCR during the course of their days and weeks at home with the kids. Most successful parents at home see the value of the TV/VCR when used with careful planning and discretion to educate and entertain. And video games, just like any other play activity, can provide kids with the opportunity to learn and develop new skills, giving them yet another chance to say, "I did it!"

## SOME TECH TIPS

**Select only high-quality programs and videos.** A good question to ask: Will the education or entertainment your child gets from watching this program be worth the time it takes him or her to watch it? In some cases the answer will be a resounding "Yes!" In other cases, you'll see fit to keep the TV off and get out the Tinker Toys instead.

**Be creative in your selections.** The TV kids like to watch isn't necessarily children's programming. For example, one friend's preschooler loves watching wildlife and nature documentaries and another's son likes to watch home improvement shows—understandable, considering that he gets to see people using tools, measuring, building decks, houses, and cabinets, and pouring cement.

**Turn it off to make turning it on an event, not a habit.** Some families design strategies for controlling their kids' viewing time, including TV tickets earned by doing chores, etc. that buy certain amounts of television time. Other families just limit the number of hours per week. I'm not too great at keeping systems like that going, so we take it day by day at our house. Regardless of the approach, it's important to practice what we preach. If we tell our children it's not good to watch too much TV but we are shouting the command above the din of a four-hour talk-show line-up we're glued to, they won't get the message.

**Watch together.** Many times, I'm the first to grab the time my children spend watching their shows to get some things done around the house. But they get the most from their TV-watching experience when I join them. As with reading, we can lift teachable moments from virtually any program. Plus, doing so reinforces the message that we care about what they're watching and that we enjoy doing things together.

# MUSIC

Music equipment (tapes/records/CDs—preferably the kind our kids can operate themselves) help us in a variety of ways:

**Mood music**—If the kids are wound up and rowdy, listening to some soothing music or a lilting story can help them settle down. On the other hand, if they're having a hard time getting any get up and go, a lively song or silly story just might put some wiggle in their waggle.

**Surrogate story spinner**—Tapes or CDs with read-along books can help save your aching throat by allowing your children to listen to their favorite stories over and over. Here's a fun way to aid long-distance grandparenting: Ask your parents and in-laws to make tapes of favorite books, then play the tapes as your kids read along.

**Music appreciation**—Exposing children to a broad range of musical experiences helps them develop a love for all kinds of music. In addition, recent studies show that exposing kids to a variety of music actually helps them to develop language, communication, and memory skills. This is also an ideal way to help your children get more from their church experience. Playing CDs of hymns, for example, help them learn the hymns and participate more fully in worship on Sunday mornings.

# Chapter 5

# your agenda: a stay-at-home mom's daily duties

> Make plans by seeking advice; if you wage war, obtain guidance. Proverbs 20:18 (NIV)

"What do you do all day?"

Ask a stay at home mom that loaded question and then run for cover. Because time and our management—or mismanagement of it—quickly become a sore spot as we consider both how slowly it can pass (the span between 4 P.M. and the time your husband's due home from work on a day when the baby's been especially fussy) and how quickly it rushes by (how much your little one has changed since just last month).

We didn't leave the workforce to micromanage our time but neither did we leave to waste it. To drift through our days without at least a general sense of direction would be to let time slip slowly and softly through our fingers . . . to the TV . . . to the phone . . . to countless other nameless distractions.

## PLANNING PAYS

Admittedly, day-planning was a tough concept for me to buy into in the rookie days of my at-home career; after all, part of the reason I wanted to be at home was to avoid rigorous schedules too often imposed by work and in classrooms. But I'm not suggesting we fill leather pocket calendars and day planners with every activity our child is to perform during each half-hour time slot between the morning's first Pop-Tart and the evening's last potty trip. I'm simply saying that, in my experience and that of most moms I've interviewed, the days  that find us rolling out of bed with a few fun ideas and a *general* plan of how we will spend our time find life moving at a nice clip. We accomplish specific goals and don't aimlessly wallow around in our pj's until noon.

Making a schedule has helped Sheryl, mom of a 1-, 3- and 5-year-old, stay on track each day. "My day rarely turns out exactly as planned," she says, "but it at least gives me a place to start. I plan trips out of the house very carefully to accomplish the maximum amount in the minimum amount of time. Just one extra, unplanned trip to Wal-Mart a week for a forgotten item can cost me greatly in terms of lost time with my family, so I try to avoid those if at all possible."

When planning your days, it helps to:

## 1. Give your day to God.

"Commit to the Lord whatever you do, and your plans will succeed" (Proverbs 16:3). In *How to Be a Motivated Christian*, author Stuart Briscoe speaks of presenting each day to the Lord as an offering. God gives it to you in the morning, you hand it back at night, thanking Him for the opportunity to use it to His glory. What you do in your daily calling is your daily worship to God. Keeping in mind this visual image of literally handing the day to God helps you to remember whose day each day really is. That practice puts a wide-angled perspective on how you spend your time.

## 2. Repeat and vary.

One important principle I learned in college under-lies all good art: Repeat pleasing elements for strength of form, then change something about them to add interest. That theory applies to almost any art form, whether it's the art of painting, writing, composing, . . . or parenting. The repetitive "busy-ness" of living each day—brushing teeth, riding bikes on the driveway, picking up toys, waiting on the front step for Daddy to come home, prayers at meals and bedtime—weaves a pattern of security and confidence into the hearts of our kids; colorful interruptions of those routines—rowdy pillow fights, watching the bulldozers clearing the vacant lot across the street, taking trips to watch the planes roar in and out of the airport—interject highlights that will spark their brightest memories.

## 3. Know your children.

Be sensitive to your kids' personalities when structuring their days. For example, it used to take Nick a while to wake up, so most days he wasn't ready for anything more active than cuddling in his sleeping bag until Scooby Doo was over. Lindsey, however, sprang from bed with a mission to milk as much fun from the day as she could, starting right then! If I wasn't ready to hand her an interesting toy first thing, she would rattle around pestering her brother instead of tackling something constructive, like figuring out how to string those play buttons onto bright strands of yarn.

## 4. Know yourself.

Whether during my first week or my 780th as a stay-at-home mom, my Tuesdays through Sundays seem out of whack unless I'm at home on Mondays. So to this day, I try not to plan outings on the first day of the week. But that may not be the way you're wired. In a nutshell, you're the boss—the supervisor of the schedule, the captain of the calendar, the director of the day planner! Arrange a work schedule that best fits your lifestyle and personality, as well as of your kids, and don't be afraid to stick to it.

# WHAT'S ON THE AGENDA?

Now let's take a look at some specific ingredients that experts—mothers and professionals alike—say make for well-rounded days in the lives of children at home.

# PLAYTIME

Playtime is much more than fun and games to a child. Research has shown that it plays a key role in a child's development of thinking, socializing, and problem-solving skills.

Although playing is crucial to children's development, experts say that knowing how to play doesn't necessarily come naturally. As parents, playing *with* our children, on their level, teaches them how to play.

Kids best enjoy their play time if you alternate activities. After quiet play, introduce rowdy play. After creative play, suggest some pretend play. To follow up educational play, allow some just-for-fun play. After indoor play, bundle up the kids and send them to the great outdoors for a while. Also, as an only child, I can vouch for the fact that solo play is special. I believe it's important to encourage spells of "solo" play to prevent "together" play among siblings or playmates from disintegrating into a sparring match—and to help kids learn how to entertain themselves.

## On-the-Job Hazard!

### Raising Too-Dependent Kids

As important as it is to play with our kids, it is equally important to encourage them to play without mom in the midst.

"A lot of times, stay-at-home moms don't train their children well enough in that area," says Cathy, mother of two and enthusiastic advocate for stay-at-home parents. "We are guilty of being so hands-on that we don't give our children the skill of playing independently.

"That's one of the biggest challenges stay-at-home moms face because we're ridden with guilt," she says. "Society says, 'You're at home, you must either be cleaning your house or entertaining your children. Otherwise, why don't you go to work?'

"I hear myself telling myself, Shouldn't you be doing this with the children? They're off having a good time, they're out in the backyard playing. They don't need me right then. But I feel compelled to be the 'perfect mother' . . . we have the tendency, I think, to overdo it."

If you've always been one to say yes to every request to play with your little ones, you may find it difficult to muster the courage to say no from time to time when you sense that independent play is in order. Try making the break gradually. Start an activity (not a game that requires two participants) with your child—one you know always captivates her attention—and after a few minutes, make an excuse to leave the room for a short time. Come back to check her progress for a few minutes, then bow out of sight a little bit longer. Pretty soon, you'll notice a big difference. She will be comfortable alone and as a result, will gain confidence and independence.

# I'M BORED!

Sometimes children get in a rut. If you're out of ideas for some different playtime activities, start an "I'm bored" envelope for each of your kids. In it, put slips of paper on which you've written some age-appropriate activities that aren't currently a part of their usual routine. The next time you hear, "I'm bored!" let your kids pull out a slip for an instant change of pace. It's easy to say no to activities that require too much preparation, hard-to-get supplies, or expense, so most of these activities are quite simple. A few, however, do require a little planning or effort—these are ideal for those days when all of you have spring fever and feel like doing something a little more elaborate.

**BALANCING ACT**—Let the kids play on a real wooden balance beam (maybe a landscape timber) or make a pretend one with chalk or masking tape.

**BALLOON PLAY**—Especially good for rainy days when you need to rustle up some rowdy indoor fun that's not too hard on the house. Kick the balloon into a laundry basket or trash can; play "hide the balloon"; tape a crepe-paper "net" across a wide doorway for some balloon volleyball (be sure the net is high enough to be a challenge).

**BEANS AND GRAINS**—A funnel, some dry beans, rice, macaroni, or oats, and a few containers add up to mounds of fun for little ones who like to fill, pour, mix, and sort (the high chair is a great place to do this, even for older tykes).

**BIKE PARADE**—Get with neighborhood kids to

decorate bikes (use balloons, crepe paper, flags, dolls, and stuffed animals) and then roll down the sidewalk in style.

**BIRD WATCHING**—Get out some binoculars and a bird book to try to identify the feathered friends in your neighborhood. Then find out what those birds like to live in and eat so you can offer room and board in your own yard.

**BLANKET SWITCH**—One mom of three keeps her kids happy by putting blankets down in different areas of the house. Each blanket is stocked with a different toy—blocks are on one, play farm on another, crayons and paper on another, etc. Each child plays on one blanket, then when the timer bell goes off every 15 minutes, they rotate.

**BLOCK BOWLING**—Set up a row of blocks, then bowl them down with any old ball or beanbag.

**BUBBLES**—They're cheap enough at the discount store, but kids always enjoy making things. Here's the recipe: $\frac{1}{4}$ cup liquid dish detergent, $\frac{1}{2}$ cup water, food coloring (optional), 1 teaspoon sugar. Mix it up then enjoy. Have bubble races or blow bubbles through a hula-hoop "goal" hung from a low branch. (For wands, save those that come in the ready-made bubbles or raid the kitchen drawers for funnels, a wire whisk, fly swatter, or baby bottle rings.)

**BUILD A VILLAGE**—From boxes, toilet paper tubes, and construction paper.

**CLOTHESPIN CONSTRUCTION**—See what silly animals and people you can make (glueless) from clothespins, markers, and fabric scraps.

**CONSTRUCT A TOWER**—From marshmallows and toothpicks.

**CREPE PAPER FUN**—Tape a finish line in a doorway or between two trees in the yard. Kids love to run through and break the ribbon.

**CROCODILE ROCK**—Play like the floor is a croc-infested swamp, and make your way across it by tossing down cardboard or cushion stepping stones. Don't fall in!

**DECORATE YOUR ROOM**—Hang a bulletin board for a kid's place to hang snapshots, Bible verses, party invitations, etc.

**DESIGN A BOARD GAME**—Use existing games for guidelines but come up with your own theme and playing pieces.

**DRAW A MURAL**—Use a large sheet of brown craft paper.

**DRESS UP**—In duds your kids make from brown paper sacks.

**DROP IT**—Cut a hole in the lid of a box and let the kids drop clothespins or other small items through the hole.

**FINGER PAINTING**—Experiment with media beyond the primary color-filled paint pots you buy at the store. Let the kids finger-paint with pudding or shaving cream on a plastic tray, a shirt box, or paper plates.

**FLASHLIGHTS**—Most kids love to play tag in the dark and try their hand at making shadow creatures.

**FOILED AGAIN**—Make a foil sculpture or hat.

**FORT TIME**—Kids like to make their own special hideouts, so give them an old sheet or a discarded appliance box to build their imaginations inside or out. Fuel the fun by letting them eat or sleep in their new constructions.

**GUESSING GAMES**—Blindfold the kids then let them "feel and guess" or "sniff and guess" the identity of items you hand them (or that you've placed in a sack). If you play the piano (even a toy one), plunk out some simple tunes and let them "name that tune." Or blindfold them and see if they can guess what's making that sound. Use bells, clocks, appliances, books, paper, instruments—anything with a distinctive noise.

**GYMNASTIC TRICKS**—Put some thick playmats or the baby bed mattress on the floor for tumbling fun.

**HIDE AND SEEK**—Timeless, for all ages. If the seeker is too young to count, let the others hide until she finishes singing her favorite song twice. For a variation, cut out plenty of brown paper sack footprints for the hider to leave as a trail for his pursuers to follow, Hansel and Gretel style. Or play sardines, having all players crowd into the hider's spot as they find it.

**HOKEY POKEY,** Looby-Loo, London Bridge, Ring around the Rosy, If You're Happy and You Know It— These fun, sing-songing games slip our minds from time to time. Ask your parents, grandparents, or in-laws what songs they sang and played when they were little.

**HOPSCOTCH**—Outdoors, sidewalk chalk the grid onto the driveway or patio; inside, use masking tape or yarn to mark the outline of the squares and numbers on the floor. Or turn a cheap vinyl tablecloth or shower curtain into a hopscotch mat by marking the game on it with a permanent marker and taping it securely to the floor with duct tape.

**HUNT FOR FOUR-LEAF CLOVERS**—Watch out for bees!

**JUMP ROPE**—How many games can you play with a jump rope? Besides the traditional activity, you can tie it up as if it were a track hurdle to jump over; you can lay it across the ground for a no-fall balance beam; you can tie it up to create a game of limbo . . . the possibilities are endless. If your memory is fuzzy about the rope-jumping chants you sang as a child, check out a book from the library or search the Internet and learn them all over again with your kids.

**LEAP FROG**—Some folks think old games like this don't appeal to today's kids. Just the opposite is true. Usually old games like this one prove the most enticing.

**MEMORY LANE**—Look through old photos and tell your child about the people, places, events (definitely something you'll want to do with your family).

**MAKEOVER MAGIC**—Set up a salon to do nails, hair and jewelry for a little princess.

**MAKE WILDFLOWER GARLANDS**—Dandelions, clover blooms, and other plentiful flowers with long, sturdy stems make terrific garlands, necklaces and bracelets. Just be careful to not pick special flowers and watch for pests like bees, mosquitoes, and poison ivy!

**MARBLE MANIA**—Tape together toilet paper and paper towel tubes to form tunnels to roll marbles through.

**MASKS**—Make silly masks from paper plates or paper grocery sacks.

**MATCHING GAMES**—Here are several simple ones: Get a new sheet of stickers and cut each sticker in half, leaving the remaining halves on the original sheets. Stick the other halves on a separate sheet of paper. Let the kids find and stick on the matching halves. Get a deck of cards and let children sort and match suits, colors, or numbers. Trace random pictures from the kids' favorite storybooks; let them find the corresponding picture in the book and then color the traced picture to match.

**MIX IT UP**—Place an assortment of dry and wet ingredients in small bowls on the kitchen table; let them concoct potions to their heart's content.

**MR. POTATO HEAD**—Play this game the old-fashioned way. Let the kids toothpick or thumbtack construction paper features onto a real spud. When they've finished, recycle the potato by cutting a design in the bottom, dipping it in paint, and stamping designs onto paper or tee-shirts.

**PLANT A GARDEN**—Let the children be in charge of watering the new plants each day.

**OBSTACLE COURSE**—Set up one using odds and ends from the garage. Jump through hula-hoops, scoot in boxes, crawl over crates, or rake balls to the finish line.

**PILLOWCASE ROMP**—Let each child stand in a pillowcase (potato-sack-race-style) for a game of chase or follow the leader. This burns up energy on rainy or cold indoor days.

**PUPPETS**—Socks, paper towel tubes, old mittens, paper sacks, and plastic spoons all make good ones. Make characters from a favorite Bible story and let the puppets act it out.

**PUZZLES**—Let the kids cut pictures from coloring books, used greeting cards, magazines or Sunday school leaflets into puzzles for each other to put together. With older kids, start a jumbo-sized jigsaw puzzle on a card table or the dining room table.

**ROADWAY**—Make a sidewalk chalk roadway in the carport, garage, or driveway where little motorists can ride their bikes, trikes, and scooters. Include familiar landmarks along the way (home, church, grandma's house, fire station, school, grocery store, etc.), as well as stop signs and traffic arrows.

**RUBBER BAND BALL**—Make a rubber band ball. It really bounces!

**SAND PLAY**—A couple of ideas: Treasure hunt—hide a few treasures (small toys or plastic eggs filled with treats) in the sandbox, then draw a treasure map to help your little ones dig up some fun. Or sift through your kitchen and bathroom drawers to find new toys to add to the sandbox—try an old wide-toothed comb, a big funnel, a few plastic straws.

**SCAVENGER HUNT**—Draw (or cut from magazines) pictures of items for your child to collect. Outdoors include pinecones, twigs, rocks, etc.; indoors, give your child a picture of all the items you see that are out of place in your home. He can collect the items, then put them where they belong. Give your child a basket, sack, or box in which to put his finds.

**SILLY SHOES**—Make shoes from shoe boxes or paper sacks (Strap them on with old shoelaces or yarn).

**SNOWBALL FIGHTS**—Even in August! Crumple up waste paper (department store sacks, used wrapping paper and tissue, or junk mail) for piles of ammunition in a safe combat zone.

**STICKERS**—Cut pictures from magazines or catalogs or draw your own. Coat back with this mixture: 2 parts white glue to 1 part white vinegar. Let dry, coat again, let dry again. Wet with sponge, then stick to paper or sticker book.

**STRAW HOUSES**—Snip plastic drinking straws and chenille wires into 2-inch pieces. Insert chenille wires into straws, then bend and build the segments into shapes.

**TALENT SHOW**—A great activity for kids of all ages. Set the stage in the living room or patio, bring out the karaoke mike and dress-up clothes, and pop some popcorn for showtime. Don't forget to charge up the video recorder and put film in the camera—you won't want to forget this!

**TARGET PRACTICE**—Hang a hula-hoop from a tree branch; take turns having water balloon (or pine cone or bouncy ball) tossing practice. Inside, hang the hula-hoop in a doorway; practice throwing paper airplanes through it.

**TOSS IT**—Pennies, buttons, pebbles, etc., can be tossed into boxes or box lids.

**TWISTER**—For a new twist on this old game, throw various shapes of colored construction paper on the floor, then call out directions geared to your child's stage of learning: "Put your hand on green" can teach body parts and colors. "Put your right foot on the rectangle" might reinforce left and right learning and shape skills; write letters and numbers on the paper for some "Put-your-left-hand-on-the-Q" fun.

**SHAVING KIT**—No need to buy gimmicky junior shave sets. Let your little ones "de-fuzz" to their hearts' content with Dad's shave cream and a craft stick razor. For smaller kids likely to get the potion in their eyes or mouth, whisk or beat tear-free baby shampoo until it's thick and foamy. Let them play barber shop or beauty shop while they're at it: Provide a water squirt bottle, combs, brushes, hair barrettes, curlers, etc.

**USE YOUR NOODLES**—Tube pasta and yarn (tape the ends for easy threading) will keep little jewelry makers busy for a while.

**WASHING DISHES**—A sturdy stool, plastic kitchenware, a dishrag, and an apron are all little ones need to wash dishes at the kitchen sink as they learn the lessons water play has to teach. For children too small to stand on a stool at the sink, put them in the high chair with a couple of soap-water-filled containers, some spoons, and a rag.

**WATER, WATER, EVERYWHERE**—Water seems to be the play ingredient of choice for preschoolers. Tiny tots can "paint" on construction paper or a brown paper sack with a brush dipped in water; older ones love to concoct all sorts of goopy potions with a container full of water and one full of flour. Bath time and, in summer, pool time, are almost always good activities as well.

# SNACK TIME

"'Nack" was one of the first words uttered out of the pouty pink mouths of each of my babies. For obvious reasons, kids typically get more excited about snack time than they do about regular mealtimes. Preparing a simple snack can reinforce creativity (decorating cookies), math skills (measuring ingredients or counting crackers), fine-motor skills (spread peanut butter), and responsibility (cleaning up). But the most valuable part of snack time is the chatter between you and your child while you're working together in the kitchen.

Need some simple snack-time ideas? Make food even more fun by using creative containers to serve up some giggles. Fill the clean or plastic-wrap-lined back of a toy dump truck with dry cereal or pretzels, arrange dainty cheese crackers on tea set dishes, or spear fruit chunks or cookies on Tinkertoy rods, drinking straws, or pick-up sticks. Look inside your kids' toy chest for more ideas.

# FOOD-TIME FUN

**APPLES**—Cut in half crosswise so the kids can see the star in the center. Spread with peanut butter (use craft-stick knives) for a healthy treat.

**APPLESAUCE**—Put three sliced apples into two cups of water. Boil, mash (let the children do this with the back of a spoon), add sugar and cinnamon to taste.

**BISCUITS & HONEY**—Let your child separate refrigerated bake-and-serve biscuits and arrange them on the pan. (Let her keep out a couple of uncooked biscuits to play with while the rest bake. If the dough gets sticky as she kneads it, just sprinkle on a little flour.) When the biscuits are ready and have cooled enough, squeeze on some honey and enjoy while reading a favorite bear tale such as Winnie the Pooh or The Three Bears. Be sure to invite your favorite teddy bears to the feast.

**BREAD AND BUTTER**—Put 1/2 pint heavy whipping cream and 1 teaspoon salt into a tightly sealed, shakable container. Shake, shake, shake while passing the time with the following rhyme. (Use craft stick knives to spread on bread or crackers.)

Come butter, come.
Come butter, come.
(Name) is at the garden gate,
Waiting for a butter cake.
Come butter, come.

(origin unknown)

**CHEERIOS**—Play this game: Put an empty container beside a container full of Cheerios. Together, count aloud how many Cheerios your child can pick up with a thin stick pretzel or toothpick and transfer into the empty container. When the fun of scooping and counting wears off, dig in! Use this chance to learn about the letter O and take a tiny bite of one to find the C and the U.

**CHEESE DIP**—It doesn't have to be the hot and spicy kind; a few melted slices of Velveeta, stirred until creamy, will do for dipping chips or cheese crackers.

**COOKIES**—Have fun with a roll of refrigerated cookie dough. Kids can pinch and drop it, spoon it, cut it with plastic knives, craft sticks, or spoon handles, or roll it and cookie-cutter it into fun (seasonal) shapes. Decorate with sprinkles or paint with colored frosting.

**GREEN EGGS AND HAM**—All it takes is a drop or two of green or blue food coloring in the eggs (before cooking) and some ham—sliced lunch-meat ham can do the trick. Note: This treat loses its effect unless you read the book while you're eating it.

**ICE POPS**—Buy some of those inexpensive make-it-yourself sets, fill with your kids' favorite drink, freeze, and enjoy. For some fun surprises with colors and flavors, see what happens when you mix lemonade with cherry Kool-Aid, etc.

**JELL-O**—Always a fun treat. Make it plain or add fruit (let the kids help chop soft fruit or tear apart orange sections). Or make the "jigglers" using the recipe on the box.

**MARSHMALLOWS**—Toasted and put on crackers with a slice of cheese; dipped in melted chocolate chips, or tossed high into the air and caught in the mouth. Experiment with other ways to eat marshmallows too.

**MINI-DOGS**—Put Vienna sausages into refrigerated bake-and-serve biscuits for an easy treat.

**PEANUT BUTTER PLAY DOUGH**—Mix 1 cup peanut butter, 3 tablespoons honey, and 1 cup nonfat powdered dry milk, then form into silly shapes before eating with a side of graham crackers or vanilla wafers.

**PEANUT BUTTER CONES**—Fill small ice-cream cones with peanut butter; let the kids dip them into Apple-Cinnamon Cheerios, finely chopped bananas, or crushed peanuts.

**POPCORN**—A stand-by favorite with kids of all ages. Serve up plain, topped with Parmesan cheese, or topped with a mixture of brown sugar and butter, then baked at a low temperature until golden and crunchy.

**PUDDING**—A fun and easy snack to make together. Just follow the instructions on the box for the shaker method. To make a simple pie, line a pie pan with graham crackers and top with the pudding, then top that with whipped topping, letting the kids do most of the work.

# REST TIME/NAP TIME

I don't know which of us at our house needs this time more, the kids or me. I need it if, for nothing else, to use the bathroom at least once a day, by myself. I also need it to recoup my space, gather my often-scattered wits, and refuel my tank before the "arsenic hour"—a phrase coined by journalist Anna Quindlen to describe the late afternoon for a mother at home with kids. Obviously, most infants take frequent or lengthy naps. Older children, however, may no longer physically need to sleep during the day. Although they would never admit it, they do need down time—the chance to simply lie down and rest, to quietly work puzzles in their rooms, or to look at books. This time will not only refresh them, but it will help them to discover and enjoy the pleasure of quiet solitude.

Even Jesus, who was God in the flesh, took time out to rest from His work. Regular quiet time helps us establish the value of rest and the concept of the Sabbath, which God gave us as a day of rest and worship. As such, naptime becomes an important way to balance the structure of our day.

# Fresh Air and Sunshine

Give kids a stick and some dirt, and they're happy for three hours. Kids run fastest, play hardest, jump farthest, laugh loudest, climb highest, and sing silliest when they're outside. And when they come inside after doing all these things, they eat a lot and sleep well.

Enough said.

# Story Time

"Read book!" toddlers command, waving chunky board books in the air. "Tell me a story!" and "Just one more!" older preschoolers plead. Preschoolers of all ages love to read books—whether it's because of the interaction with Mommy, the sound of the words, the bright and interesting pictures, the story itself, or a combination.

Wise mommies and experts alike know that the most rewarding story time experiences involve much more than reading words and turning pages. Think how much more vividly the children see the story of the three bears when we use our biggest, booming voice for the daddy bear, a shaky falsetto for the momma bear, and a squeaky baby voice for baby bear. I've turned into quite a drama queen in the privacy of my own read-aloud endeavors, fueled by the giggles and squeals of my small but adoring audience. When your kids are small, try not to rush into focusing on words and letters. Spend time on the pleasures of rhythm and color of the language and the thrill of suspense. Taking your time with story time will teach your little ones the pleasures of a good book.

# SOCIALIZATION

One of the comments often made by mothers at home concerns the social lives of our kids. Well-meaning cousin Myrtle will insist that 13-month-old Caleb needs to have some playmates. The nice woman down the street audibly pities your 2-year-old because she doesn't have anyone to play with—after all, the other kids in the neighborhood her age are in day care.

However, studies show that as long as parents realize the need for social interaction, children raised at home can become well-adjusted social creatures. While your 2-year-old may not be ready for an organized playgroup, your 3-year-old might be ready for playmates.

It's one thing to determine when your kids are ready to make their social debut; it's another to figure out where to recruit playmates. A logical place to begin the search is in your church family, where children may gradually become playmates with their former nursery or Sunday school classmates. Outside the church, logical places to scout out some play pals include your family, your neighborhood, your circle of friends who have children the same ages as yours, Mother's Day Out programs, the local library's story hour, and organized play groups.

# FIELD TRIPS

The phrase "field trip" conjures dozens of long-forgotten, school-day images: bright yellow buses, perfumed homeroom mothers, the buddy system, the free feeling of being somewhere besides school between 8 a.m. and 3 p.m. But field trips for children at home start long before grade school. They happen sometimes on a daily basis, and they're often as simple as going to the grocery store—if we'll adopt a field trip attitude along the way.

Seize the unique opportunity you have as a parent at home to give your kids a running commentary about the world around them as you get out in it and explore it together. For example, as you're driving to the grocery store some afternoon, you might pass the postal worker, a gas truck delivering gas to the corner filling station, and a woman in a wheelchair at an intersection. As you get out of the car at the store, you see a cement truck crew pouring a new section of the parking lot as a jet roars overhead. Not only can you point out all these sights and sounds, but you can use each as the starting point for educational and fun discussion that will help your kids learn more about their world. I'm not talking about launching into encyclopedic lectures on jet propulsion. I'm simply suggesting that you ask a few questions to prompt curiosity and sharpen observation skills. Your children will learn much more about their world when they are trained to see what is around them.

Read the paper, watch the news, be aware of local happenings that might interest your kids. Circus trains roll into town, a children's theater troupe plays at local spots, military bases stage air shows, communities host festivals, business owners hold public relations events with clowns, balloons, and sometimes even special appearances by kids' favorite costumed characters.

Take the long way home. Some of my best childhood memories go like this: We would leave church on Sunday afternoon and my dad would head home the usual way, until we got about halfway there. Then he would take a surprise turn. "Where are we going?" I would ask. "Oh, I just thought we'd take the long way home," he would say casually. We might just see some different houses in some different neighborhoods. That was nice. Or we might pass a dairy diner that would catch Daddy's eye. That was even better. And we might even pass a shopping center with a parking lot carnival in progress. That was best of all. You never know what you'll discover when you take the long way home. That's why it's so much fun.

Be spontaneous. This must be a factor in all of the above ideas or they will lose their engaging touch. Passing the carnival on the way home would have been just another sight if Daddy had said, "We can't stop because I have to go home and mow the yard."

# LET'S GO!

Take a look at the following free or inexpensive field trip suggestions. You might have to muster your networking and assertiveness skills to gain access to some of these destinations. If you homeschool, join with other homeschooling families in your area for an outing. If you don't, consider asking a few of your fellow stay-at-home moms and their kids to go along.

**AIRPORT**—Watch planes landing and taking off, luggage trains caterpillaring across the tarmac, and ground crews preparing planes for their next flights. Do some serious people-watching. An airport is a great place to talk about emotions: Ask your little ones why some people at the airport are sad and some people are happy. It's also a good spot to sharpen observation, imagination, and logic skills: "Where do you think they have been?" you might ask about a deeply tanned couple with shorts, hiking boots, and backpacks. Or "Where do you think she is going?" you could ask about a sharply dressed woman carrying a briefcase.

**ARTIST'S STUDIO**—To find one, ask friends in design, advertising, or public relations. Talk about sparking a child's creativity—seeing adults who make their living drawing, sculpting, and painting gives new value to the kids' kitchen-table endeavors.

**BAKERY**—Be sure to sample some of the products!

**BIG BUILDINGS DOWNTOWN**—Ride the escalators and elevators, talk about the different businesses you see, and check out a sky-high view to give your kids a new perspective of their city.

**AUTO BODY SHOP**—Kids love to watch grown-ups fix things; this is the perfect place to do that while taking in lots of other sights, sounds, and smells as well.

**BRIDAL SHOP**—After a visit here, go home and

play wedding by dressing up in the fanciest clothes (and sheets and scarves) you can find! If you have a recording or photos of your own wedding, this would be a great time to dust them off and show the kids.

**CHURCH**—Ask your pastor to guide you and your children on a tour of your church. Have him explain the areas and the furnishings in each area. Let your child get a close-up look at the organ, at stained-glass windows, and similar places. This is a great way to help your children grow in their understanding of God's house and worship. Come Sunday, they will be much more attentive and participatory.

**DAIRY**—At the ones near my home in Arkansas, tours are routine, so you get a great learning experience as well as a sample of ice cream in the hospitality room on the way out.

**FARM**—If you have a friend or relative with a farm, go there as often as you politely can! Animals, open spaces, tractors, barns, hay, ponds, ducks . . . this is the place we've grown up singing about.

**FIRE STATION**—Field trips don't get much more exciting than this. Our car happened to break down in front of a fire station close to our home, and we went inside to call for help. For weeks afterward, Nick talked about his peek inside the firehouse and his close-up view of the fire truck.

**HOSPITAL**—If kids are allowed, go to look at the new babies. Talk about when your kids were newborn in the hospital, and then go home and get their newborn pictures out so they can see how much they've changed and grown.

**LIBRARY**—Ask your children's librarian about story time, video series for kids, reading clubs, and other child-oriented events. But you don't, of course, need a planned event for a fun library trip. Get a library card and just find the children's section where the kids can browse to their hearts' content.

**MOVIES**—Go the budget route at discount matinees or dollar theaters. Check the sale bins at your favorite video rental store.

**MUSEUMS**—Call to find out whether they have any hands-on activities or special programs suited to the ages of your kids.

**NEWSPAPER**—There's always a lot going on in the newsroom of even the smallest of papers; they're used to giving tours and often have souvenirs to send home with the little ones.

**NURSING HOME**—Check your church's roster for members living at nursing homes who might like a visit. Don't go empty-handed; take a bottle of lotion, some stationery and stamps, something good to eat (be sure to see about dietary restrictions), a handmade greeting card, or a cheerful plant to brighten the room.

**PARK**—Picnic, play, people-watch!

**PET STORE**—Find out whether someone who works there can tell your kids about how they get the animals and how they care the different kinds of animals sold there. Seek out the most unusual critter and then go home and find out more about it on the Internet or in an encyclopedia.

**PLAYS**—A children's theater, a university drama department, or a high school drama club might be planning a production your kids would love; check newspapers or call around for information.

**POLICE STATION**—Even a glimpse into a police car is a thrill for many kids.

**RESTAURANT**—The kid kind, with burgers, chicken, or pizza—and a playground—is an old standby for a rainy day.

**WORK**—Daddy's, grandparents', friends'. Kids love a behind-the-scenes look at the places where their loved ones work.

**ZOO**—If you have help with the kids, video the whole excursion, beginning to end, for hours of at-home video watching fun. It's also fun to play zoo bingo. Prepare for each child cards featuring a bingo-style grid of animal pictures or stickers. Give each player a sheet of stickers for the markers, and go to it. First one to complete a row gets to choose the picnic table at lunch!

# CLEANING HOUSE: DO I REALLY HAVE TO?

Many of us were raised in the generation of women who weren't required to take home economics in high school. As little girls, we may have draped ourselves over our moms' shoulders as they sat at their sewing machines, hummed along with the monotone song of their vacuum cleaners, or snatched licks of frosting from dripping beaters. But we may not have bothered to take notes on the mechanics of these activities as we watched our moms because the women's movement was spurring many of us toward "higher callings." Résumés, business suits, and briefcases were to become our accouterments—not feather dusters, rubber gloves, and mop buckets.

But now we're home. The dates on our résumés have expired, our plastic-covered suits hang in the rear of the closet, and we've donated our briefcases to our kids' baskets of dress-up clothes. Mothering has become our career; housework, an integral part of that career if for no other reason than simple logic: we're at home anyway, so why not do some chores and make dinner? However, housework is a part of our new vocation that many of us only reluctantly embrace because of some common attitudes that fuzz our approach toward it, making the H word more of a problem than it really ought to be. Here they are, along with some ideas about how to bust them.

# BUSTING FUZZ

### Fuzzball #1:
### I'll clean the house,
### but I won't enjoy doing it.

At the risk of sounding like a third-grade Bible drill captain, I offer the following:

"Whatever you do, work at it with all your heart, as working for the Lord, not for men." (Colossians 3:23)

Notice, this does not begin with "whatever you do that you really like to do."

"God loves a cheerful giver." (2 Corinthians 9:7)

Aren't we "giving" continually as homemakers? Giving our time, our talents, our energy.

"Do everything without complaining or arguing." (Philippians 2:14)

Again, not "do just the fun things without grumbling or disputing."

Why do we try to teach our little ones to do what we ask of them cheerfully, without protest, when we so often are the ones who teach them how to gripe?


### Fuzzball #2:
### I'm above doing housework.

You may feel like mothering is a noble enough calling to merit quitting a full-time career, but housework doesn't shine nearly as honorably. It's easy to slip into a huffy "I-can't-believe-this-is-what-I-went-to-college-for" attitude, especially when tackling some of the most unsavory household chores: scrubbing the shower, washing dishes, putting away laundry, cleaning the toilet—again. But let's face it: Most of us who previously held paying jobs had to handle at least a few thankless or just plain nasty chores. Had I told my editor at the paper that opening the day's mail, looking up a hard-to-find article from a back issue, or watering the department's drooping plant wasn't in my job description, he probably would have told me to take a long hike. The attitude of not wanting to serve others is just human nature at work. We need to fight against that attitude and learn to imitate Christ, who came to this earth not to be served but to serve.

Remember the passage from John 13 when Jesus washes the disciples' feet? In those days, this task was reserved for slaves. Yet Jesus said, "Now that I, your Lord and Teacher, have washed your feet, you also should wash one another's feet. I have set you an example that you should do the same as I have done for you. I tell you the truth, no servant is greater than his master" (John 13:14–16). We are called to our vocation as stay-at-home-parents and to all the tasks it requires. Performing such tasks, even the unsavory ones, is one of the ways we glorify God.

### Fuzzball #3:
### I'm not good at keeping house, so why bother?

Why bother? Because God desires that "everything should be done in a fitting and orderly way" (1 Corinthians 14:40). Take note: He doesn't say, "Let all things be done immaculately and in alphabetical order."

(If that were the case, we would all become too discouraged to ever pick up a dust rag.) But, thankfully, that verse tells us to simply do what it takes to make life in our households run on as smooth a track as possible. For some of us, "fitting and orderly" might mean we can pick up the newspaper from the kitchen counter without something sticky grabbing and tearing the bottom page. For others, it might mean wiping the sand and grit out of the bathtub with the same towel that just blotted the kids dry. Our housekeeping standards and styles vary. Develop a set of realistic housekeeping goals that make you and your family comfortable.

## Fuzzball #4:
### Keeping house with young children in it is impossible.

The fact that we're home all day every day with kids who are virtual mess factories compounds our frustration that even when we manage to get the house clean, we can't manage to keep it clean. Fueling the fire are well-intended books and magazine articles suggesting we get our priorities in order by hiring someone to clean our homes so we can spend more time with the kids. Financial reality rings loud and clear: For many mothers at home, hiring household help just isn't in the budget.

But take it from many moms at home: It is possible to keep a home with young kids in residence at least reasonably clean, especially if we organize, create a workable plan, and delegate.

**ORGANIZE**—Get rid of as much clutter as possible and arrange your home in the most logical (not always the traditional) fashion.

**CREATE A WORKABLE PLAN**—Routines save time as well as the energy of having to decide what to do when each day.

**DELEGATE**—When a friend was expecting her third child, I marveled at how efficiently she managed to run her home despite round-the-clock morning sickness and two rambunctious preschool boys underfoot. She gave her kids the credit because she had already taught them how to do the basics like fold and put away clothes, dress themselves, answer the phone politely, and help with other household tasks. This helped her tremendously when she wasn't feeling up to par, and it instilled in her boys a sense of responsibility as well as the satisfaction of accomplishment.

Even if your kids aren't ready to take on complete responsibility for household chores, they might surprise you by their willingness to at least help. Some housekeeping tricks include:

✳ Give each kid a rag to help dust wood furniture and paper towels to help clean glass doors and mirrors.

✳ Let them blaze a trail by picking up toys, rugs, and fuzz in front of the vacuum cleaner's path.

✳ Give them a wet rag to wash their toys and shelves while you're changing their bedding and cleaning their rooms.

❋ Hand them wet clothes from the washer to put into the dryer.

❋ Let them load and unload unbreakable dishes from the dishwasher.

❋ Let them set the unbreakables at the table: place mats, napkins, condiments in plastic bottles, etc.

❋ Let them use their toy housekeeping implements along with you: popcorn vacuums, little broom, play kitchen, etc.

❋ Scramble up pairs of shoes as you empty closet floors to vacuum them, then let the kids match the pairs as they reload the closet floor.

❋ Let them mist plants with the sprayer while you water.

❋ Let them help sort clothes by color (reds, whites, darks) and fold and stack the laundry coming out of the dryer.

### Fuzzball #5:
#### Housework isn't really that important.

Oh, yes it is—to an extent! Chances are that domestic order figured into the picture, if not near the top, then at least in the top 10 goals you penned back in the first chapter. Why is it so important?

You may want to make your home a clear contrast to the hectic, messy, and disorganized world beyond your driveway. You want clean floors if for no other reason than because your toddler would just as soon eat off the floor as off dishes. And although your walls may sport a cute plaque with a folksy rhyme about excusing messes while you rock your baby, you wonder how comfortable your guests would really feel if they were to crunch crumbs from last night's dinner as they walked across the kitchen floor.

In addition, you may find it difficult to imagine that the ideal woman, whose portrait is painted in Proverbs and whose standard we strive toward, had a basin full of dirty pottery, overflowing garbage baskets, or less-than-fresh straw in her family's bedding.

However, balance is the key. God calls us as parents to bring reasonable order into their lives. Yet while we do need to clean our homes, we need more urgently to rock our children while they're still rockable, tell stories while they want to listen, and impart the message of Martha and Mary. To forego the blessings of the Lord's presence in our living rooms, in the hearts of our beautiful kids, and in the vocation we've been called to lead would be to settle for second best.

We try to do everything we need to do. We try to be the very best parents we know how to be. Sometimes we fall short. When that happens, we can listen to the words of the psalmist: "Be still and know that I am God. . . . The LORD of hosts is with us; the God of Jacob is our fortress" (Psalm 46:10–11). We can take refuge in the Word of God and in His forgiveness, mercy, safety— and peace.

# On-the-Job Hazard!

### Haggling Over Housework

Once you begin staying home, your husband may take that as a green light to turn the household chores he has been taking care of over to you. Or you may assume that since you're at home all the time now, the entire responsibility for keeping house should be yours.

"My husband helped more when we were both working," said Lana, mother of two. "After I started staying home, I felt like I should be doing the lion's share of the housework and he didn't put up much of a fight."

Whether it's your idea or his that you become chief housekeeper once you return home, it's not often a very good idea. Talk with your husband about ways to continue splitting the chores—if not 50–50, at least in a way that will help you make sure you continue to get your priorities met. Lana says that while she still has some housekeeping issues, she began to resolve some of the conflict first, by "realizing that I am not going to have a perfect house at this stage in my life (if ever);" and second, by learning "what parts of the housework I have to stay on top of to keep my own sanity."

# staying home

"When my first was born, I almost immediately calculated how many years I would have to wait to return to the work force," she says. "I repeated the same calculations when my second arrived two years later."

But "my oldest started preschool last year, and I'm happy to say that I have no intention of returning to an office outside of my home! Ever!"

Chapter 6

# your tenure: stay-at-home moms staying at home

> Let us not grow weary in doing good, for at the proper time we will reap a harvest if we do not give up. (Galatians 6:9)

"Free at last, free at last!"

Many tired moms feel like shouting as the bright yellow school bus pulls away from the curb to tote their last-born to the first day of kindergarten.

This day, after all, marks the end of an era for lots of women who exited the career track to be at home full-time only until their children reached school age. They marched into stay-at-home motherhood knowing their mission on the home front would be short-term.

Now they are ready to unearth the briefcase from the back of the closet, polish up their pumps, and rejoin the ranks of the paid full-time workforce.

Statistics show these moms are in the majority. Nearly 70 percent of married couples with school-age children (between the ages of 6 and 17) were both employed outside the home in 1997, and that number continues to grow each year. A 2000 Census Bureau report indicates that 7 million American latch-key kids ages 5–14 go home to empty houses after school each day because both parents work during those hours.

But some moms opt to remain home for yet a few more years, some even indefinitely, either by staying out of the paid workforce altogether or by seeking flexible schedules that enable them to take an active daytime role in their children's schools and to be home for the kids after school.

## BEING THERE

Catie, mother of two, says she decided to remain at home after her children started school because she wants to simply *be there* for her kids. "Being around whenever my kids need me, not when my job allows," she says, "is a priceless benefit no company can offer!"

The decision, she says, was not one she had expected to make.

"When my first was born, I almost immediately calculated how many years I would have to wait to return to the work force," she says. "I repeated the same calculations when my second arrived two years later."

But "my oldest started preschool last year, and I'm happy to say that I have no intention of returning to an office outside of my home! Ever!"

For moms like Gina, the desire to remain at home for son Bradley and daughter Melody through their school-age years didn't come as a surprise. Rather, she never for a moment planned to reenter the workforce because she always recognized that her children "have even greater needs for me when they are in school. I want to be able to be involved in their school and other activities," she says. "I don't think I could juggle it all and work outside the home, too." Many other moms remain in the stay-at-home mom category even after the kids reach school age because of their strong convictions to home school.

Although continuing to forego career for kids may not be the right choice—or even an option—for everyone, parents who make that decision generally do so because they believe stay-at-home motherhood is the best forum for guiding their kids through the school-age years.

"I worked when my kids were babies, but have since come home to work and felt like the time was right, now that they are in school—for lots of reasons," says Louise, mom of two. "They are so busy! They are in piano and dance, t-ball and swimming. I felt so guilty not being the one to be at their events, to support them, get them there, help with their anxieties, deal with a forgotten ball glove. They have needs that are very different now that they are in school: making friends, making choices, homework. I miss working, but feel very blessed to be here—especially when they walk in the door after school. I am the first person they see and the first person they tell about their day."

Corin, mother of twins, agrees. "I think almost every stage after birth is a crucial one as far as being able to stay home with your child," she says, "but my convictions for working at home in order to be there for my twins have never been stronger as when they started kindergarten. . . . Because I'm a work-at-home mother, I am able to volunteer in their classrooms about once a week. This gives me a rare and privileged opportunity to see how they are in this setting, and how I as a parent can help in their progress and academic and social development stages. . . . Not only am I able to volunteer in the classroom, but every day when they get home from school, I am there to make them lunch, talk about their day, go over homework, and basically just reinforce the morning's learning process while it's still fresh."

# BIGGER KIDS, BIGGER CHALLENGES

But lest you think the later years of stay-at-home mothering will be a cinch, think again. The years when the kids' teeth are falling out can be as trying as the months when they were coming in. The days when the kids are in school can be just as busy, if not busier, than when you had them in your nest all the time. (Or, if you home school, the school age years mean your days will be fuller than ever!)

From "Watch me write 'pickle' in cursive!" and

"guess how many marshmallows I can fit in my mouth!" to "What do you do when you're in heaven?" and "Why does God let those bad guys run around?" school-age kids can bewilder parents with their demands for attention, time, energy, moral guidance, and information.

Although moms of the physically sufficient set may be expecting to reclaim more of the personal time and independence our infants and toddlers strip from us, we soon learn that older children come equipped with a set of just-as-demanding needs.

For example, their sense of spirituality begins to sharpen, prompting "out there" questions and a need for a perceptive parent's eyes and ears. They are beginning to understand the huge concept of the sacrifice Jesus Christ made for them and to try to sort through some of the weighty matters Christians face in a post-modern world. Yet their emotional maturity on any given day can dramatically tumble from even-tempered to volatile, or well-adjusted to ultrasensitive, requiring a delicately balanced mixture of tenderness, wisdom, firmness, humor, and sometimes a handful of homemade chocolate chip cookies. Their social lives begin to blossom, intruding into time we used to call our own and putting us behind the wheel more than we've ever been in our lives. That sparks the need for our flexibility, diplomacy, and tact. And if that's not enough, the daily news deluges us with issues we must decide if/when/how to discuss with our inquisitive young citizens. Questions about education, sex, extracurricular activities, violence, safety, and budding independence make our worries just a few years ago about nursing, teething and diaper rash seem like, well, child's play by comparison.

"Developing their understanding of God, [and what's] right and wrong in the world these days" is one of the most formidable challenges Judy, mother of two, admits she faces in her job as a stay-at-home mom.

Another tricky task comes as we try to give each child what he or she needs, individually, as our families grow with the addition of younger siblings. In fact, mothers in larger families often say much stress comes from trying to meet the specialized needs of each of their children. "My biggest challenges are being able to be involved with all three kids' classes, accomplishing all the homework each day, and keeping up with each child's schedule," says Tula, whose children range in age from 5 to 12.

Andrea also says she finds it tough to divide her time and attention among her three sons. "It's hard sometimes to keep everybody balanced," she says.

The thing about raising older kids is that we can't always use the tricks we relied on to care for them when they were babies. We can no longer put them on the floor with some blocks, sing them a lullaby, or plunk them down in the sandbox to play. But that's not to say we can't enter this phase of parenting equipped with some strategies that will help us continue to celebrate stay-at-home motherhood as our children grow. On the contrary, gearing up for some of the issues school-age parenting brings our way—which is what we'll do in the next few chapters—can help us savor these days of dance recitals, sleepovers, and tennis shoes as much or more as we do during the days of first steps, bedtime stories, and baby booties.

# Chapter 7

# a promotion! surviving & thriving during school "daze"

> But His mother treasured all these things in her heart. Luke 2:38

Swallowing sobs as I made my way through the blurred parking lot after leaving Nick in a room full of strangers on his first day of kindergarten, I didn't feel I would ever be able to climb out from under the blanket of grief smothering me. I wasn't mourning the big issues many journalists write about in touching back-to-school columns in thick, slick magazines and Sunday newspapers: I didn't feel my firstborn wasn't going to need me anymore—I remembered enough about being a school-ager to know you never quit needing mom. I didn't worry about my diminishing role in his world. I wanted him to have a circle of friends—and I knew I planned to continue to be enough of a hands-on mom that I wouldn't yield my influence on him for a long time to come. And I wasn't simply feeling sentimental in the "where did the time go . . . just yesterday I was bringing him home from the hospital" sense. I had, after all, become a stay-at-home mom to prevent ever having to say such a thing. I knew good and well where the time had gone. He had spent it with me, day after day, being rocked and raised, discipled and disciplined in his home, in his yard, at his pace and according to his personality. I was sending him off to school knowing I had given him the very best—and most—of what I had to offer during the years I had him in my complete care. What's more, I trusted that the God who cares for the birds of the air and the flowers in the field would also care for my little one.

No, the source of my grief was much more basic: I was just going to miss him so much. The little boy who had rocked my world and shaken our family's priorities into place five years earlier would no longer be folding bomber planes at 10 a.m. or building forts in the den after a chicken nugget lunch. He wouldn't be holding Lindsey's other hand as the three of us walked into the grocery store to do our shopping. He wouldn't be spouting out colorfully turned "Nickabulary" words and phrases throughout the day that would send me running to my little blue notebook where I record them.

He would be parked at his desk in the kid-colored classroom, sponging up new info about his world, making Pilgrim hats and terrariums, and monkeying around on the playground while his three-year-old sister and I tried to sort out a new structure for our lives. We were Nick-less, and it felt just awful.

I wish I could say that a life-changing revelation came later that day to dissolve my grief. Or that the replay was easier two years later when Lindsey became a kindergartner. Or this past year—in fact, just as I was putting the finishing touches on this manuscript—when Erin crossed the bridge between preschool to big kid school. But I can't. The drama of separating from kids we've spent practically every hour with since they were born can't be downplayed.

I can, however, say this: we adjust. I'm sure some moms do so more quickly than others. For me, the grief creeps away in small degrees as I discover that back-to-school isn't synonymous with total separation and that, hey, it feels pretty good to have more time to call my own.

As I came out of the fog of sadness that first time, I began to see clearly that this transition was signaling a promotion in my career of stay-at-home motherhood. My kids were being launched from their home pad to explore the "real world." I was blasting off alongside them into a mothering job that carried extra duties, an expanded territory, and an ever-increasing crew of colleagues that now included not just other moms but teachers and faculty, gym instructors and baseball coaches. This advancement called for sharp people-management skills, acute attention to details, a knack for time-management, a capacity for multi-tasking, and a thorough knowledge of problem-solving techniques.

So, intimidated as I was by the promotion, for the

second time in my mothering career I decided to do some on-the-job training. I found out everything I could to master the basics of school-age parenting.

# GETTING READY FOR SCHOOL

Whether the kids are starting kindergarten or fourth grade, sliding from summertime into public or private school can be both a joyful and a jarring experience. Here are some off-to-school do's and don'ts that will prevent mental meltdown as we prepare ourselves, our kids, and even our homes, for the big change:

**DO:**

**Establish a regular bedtime** at least a week, preferably two, before school starts.

**Practice the getting-up and getting-ready routine** at least a few days before D-day (a cool new alarm clock for each school-bound child might be a great back-to-school present).

**Begin "selling" school** by mentioning things to look forward to. ("The kindergartners always go to the pumpkin patch in the fall . . . won't that be fun?" "Can you believe this is the year you will start learn-

ing to read?" "Third-grade classes get to take turns at
flagpole duty.")

**Discuss getting to school.** If you'll be carpooling,
go over all the details of who's driving and on what
days. Make sure your children can easily recognize
the other carpool drivers' vehicles in the parking lot
or traffic lanes. If your kids will be riding the bus, visit
the bus stop and go over details of the entire bus
experience. Find out the driver's name, the bus number, which friends will be riding the bus. Go over
bus/traffic safety rules.

**Take care of dental, eye doctor, and pediatric
check-ups** before school begins. We made the mis-
take of putting off Lindsey's eye exam too long—and,
as a result, she got her first pair of glasses right at
the beginning of kindergarten ... two unsettling
changes for a five-year-old to handle at once.

**Start setting up the school zones:** hang hooks by
the back door for backpacks, set up files or notebooks to catch each kids' notes, permission slips, etc.;
designate drawers or boxes to collect each child's
keepsake work.

**Review names and numbers your kids should
remember**—home, Dad at work, Grandma, carpool
drivers. (For younger ones, print the info on an index
card, laminate it, and attach it to their backpack.)

**Review last year's (if you have one) yearbook**
to remind your kids of familiar faces and names.

**Get your lunch plan ready.** Talk to lunch takers
about what they'll like packed in their lunch, and
gather plastic bags, napkins, straws, and milk money

into one corner of the kitchen to save steps. Talk to your novice cafeteria tray eaters about how to carry a loaded tray through a crowd of kids (practice in your own kitchen if they're nervous), and go over the school's lunchtime routine.

**Start a habit of laying out tomorrow's clothes** the night before.

**Make school preparations fun and special:** plan a mother-daughter school clothes shopping trip; set up a special box to collect school supplies purchased throughout the summer; start a tradition of picking out a new backpack or lunchbox every even or odd year.

**Talk about how you plan to be involved at school** if you're not teaching the kids at home. ("I'll be helping Mrs. Johnson in the library each Wednesday," or "I'm going to be Mrs. Cook's room mother this year.")

**Set up your school-mom station.** Keep a note pad, pen, envelopes, and a few dollars and quarters in one spot at the kitchen desk to jot notes to teachers, sign permission slips, rustle up popcorn money, and fill out school portrait and book orders.

**Designate a drawer, expandable file folder, or a box for each child's papers, notes, and schedules.** You'll know right where to go when you need the receipt showing you paid for your son's yearbook or when you want to have another look at your daughter's last mid-term report to see what areas she needs help in.

## DON'T:

**Emphasize how much you'll miss your kids** during the days

**Express worry or complain about certain teachers** ("I sure hope you don't get Mrs. Weasel. I hear she yells a lot.")

**Make light of comments that reveal your kids' concerns**—encourage them to talk about their worries and guide them to possible solutions to their anticipated problems

**Over schedule after-school time**

**Plan unusual or potentially disruptive activities early in the year** (this isn't the time to schedule your non-emergency foot surgery, for example)

## On-the-Job Hazard!

### A Painful Separation

I flunked the "smooth transition into kindergarten" test with my first two kids. The fact is, physically and emotionally separating a mother and child for the first time after five years of practically nonstop companionship can be like trying to pull apart two sheets of paper that are glued together. There are going to be a few tears in each piece of paper. Only in this case, we didn't see "tears," as in torn paper; we saw "tears," as in crying at the beginning of each day of kindergarten. They would cry at the classroom door as I pried their arms from around my waist and handed them over to their teachers; I would cry in the van in the parking lot because I hated that they were starting their day with sadness.

This went on for months, and in the case of one child (I better not share which one because they say I embarrass them enough in my writing projects as it is), occasional episodes of tears continued into first grade. The teachers and I never could correlate the crying to a specific cause other than, "he/she would just rather be home instead of here." If I ever had a time of doubt about whether I had done the right thing by staying home with my kids, this was that time. For a while I began to think I had done them no favors by staying home to raise them because sending them out into the real world was proving to be far too traumatic! My attempts to help—from tough love and tenderness to talking and treats—did nothing to make the start of their days any easier. But eventually, in their timing, the good starts began to outnumber the bad starts until, finally, there were no more tears.

In hindsight I realize I could have made separation easier by enrolling them in a mother's day out program or by taking them to friends' homes to play more often during their preschool years. So when Erin came along, I deliberately took those steps. She grew up spending more time away from me when she was three and four years old, so her transition into kindergarten went much more smoothly. There were no tears this time. (At least, not from her. As it turned out, I produced enough for the both of us once the realization hit me that my last baby was leaving the nest!)

# THE HOME-SCHOOL CONNECTION COUNTS

Plainly put, kids whose parents plug into their kids' education do better in school. They perform better on standardized tests, adjust better socially, report higher levels of self-confidence, excel in math and science . . . the list goes on. Here are some ways to strengthen our link to our kids' learning experiences:

## 1. Team Up With Teachers

As kids hop off school buses and tumble out of minivans on the first day of school, they aren't the only ones wondering what the next nine months hold. Behind each backpack-clad student stands an anxious mom or dad wondering the same thing.

As for me, I am certain of this: At the beginning of each school year, I get ready to fall in love again.

No, I don't chuck my values—or my husband—out the window to run away to the Bahamas with the cable guy. I just know from years of experience that I tumble head over heels for my kids' teachers.

My little romance with teachers began in my own second-grade classroom, when jolly Mrs. White tickled her snaggle-toothed bunch of seven-year-olds into hysterics by colorfully defining the manure we were spreading on our vegetable garden. Other highlights of this amour have included a fascinated crush on Mrs. Miles, a Native American who gave my fourth-grade class ukulele lessons, and respectful adoration of Ms. Molett, a stern but loving nun who taught in public schools "way back when" it was okay to read a Bible verse to her class each morning.

As an adult, I had nearly forgotten about my tendency to fall in love with teachers until always-smiling Mrs. Jessup rekindled the flame by ushering my first-grader across the life-changing threshold between "can't read" and "can read." Suddenly my inquisitive, blue-eyed six-year-old wasn't asking me to read to him; he was reading to ME!

To keep the sparks of romance crackling in our parent-teacher relationships, we can use some of the same tips that sustain a healthy marriage:

**AVOID COMPARISONS:** I don't react well when my husband says, "That's not how my mom always cooked spaghetti." So rather than screeching, "Mrs. Bailey always used to let Lindsey . . . ," we should guard our mouths tongues to keep from calamity (Proverbs 21:23).

**SHOW RESPECT:** Although some may not appear old enough to drive themselves to school each day (and they look younger every year!), teachers have worked hard to acquire an education and earn their spot at the head of the class. We should hand them the reins of our kids' education, submit ourselves and our kids "for the Lord's sake" to their authority, and give them the respect that God intends for us to show everyone (1 Peter 2:13, 17). When a problem does crop up—and it likely will at some point— rather than whining to fellow moms or destroying the teacher's trust by heading straight for the principal's office, we should first discuss it with the teacher, offering any possible solutions we see. We're likely to get a much speedier and more effective resolution when we don't alienate the teacher.

**MAKE DATES:** Dates with our mates allow us to reflect on our past and chart our future course. Dates with teachers—disguised as both parent-teacher conferences and impromptu discussions after school or during field trips—give us occasion to celebrate our kids' accomplishments and to strategize ways to reach educational goals.

"I try to keep very active lines of communication going between my son's teacher and me," says Gina. "I talk with her frequently ... not just at parent-teacher conferences."

Some conversation-starters for productive teacher conferences include:

* What has my child been learning and what will he or she be expected to learn in the coming weeks?

* How is my child evaluated—how are grades determined?

* What can I do at home to complement class work?

* What can I do to help in the classroom?

* Does my child need any special help such as speech therapy, tutoring, accelerated programs, etc., that I should check into?

When we need to discuss several issues with the

teacher, a list of notes can help make sure we cover everything. And we should remember to approach these one-on-ones not just as information gatherers, but as information givers as well. This is the ideal setting to share personal info that can help the teacher cue into our student's needs. Now is the time to mention that Charlie gets bored when he finishes his work early; that Maddie's self-confidence has blossomed since the teacher gave her the responsibility of being this week's office runner. Also pass along vital personal information—a death in the family, job change, illness, best friend moving away, etc.—can cause our children to act differently in school. Letting teachers in on these developments can help them better help our kids.

> **WRITE LOVE LETTERS:** With a job description almost as long and varied as that of a parent, teachers can always use the pen-and-paper equivalent of a pat on the back. So when they do special things for our kids—whether they spend a few extra minutes to teach subtraction, pull a wobbly tooth, or give a comfort hug to help conquer a teary bout with the Monday morning blues—we can take a few minutes to drop them a hearty "way to go!"

> **GIVE TOKENS OF ESTEEM:** Teachers often spend more than a little of their own pocket money on their class in various ways throughout the year. And that's not to mention the valuables they spend that aren't monetary: time, effort, care, concern, prayer. A little gift now and then can help show our appreciation for their beyond-the-call of duty deeds. And just like a little something from our spouse at times other than birthday and anniversary can bright-

en any day, that spontaneity can do the trick for a tired teacher as well. Here are some tips for expressing your thankfulness:

✳ Ask fellow teachers for ideas about special interests.

✳ Pick up some note cards/stamps.

✳ Consider pooling resources with other parents for more expensive items: gift certificate to the school supply store or catalog, set of books, etc.

✳ Find out what the teacher would like to have in the classroom that isn't in the budget—an electric pencil sharpener, computer software, a couple of beanbag chairs for the reading area, a certain set of reference books, for example.

✳ Offer to take over her lunchtime playground duty once a month.

✳ Assemble a basket of personal goodies—bath salts, lotions and potions; herbal teas and flavored coffees; nail care supplies.

✳ Let your child decorate/personalize a canvas tote bag.

✳ Purchase a classic video for her home library.

✳ Give homemade, handcrafted items.

✳ Share food (canned goodies, fresh-baked cookies) in a pretty reusable tin.

✳ Send a potted plant for the teacher's classroom or home.

✻ Cut flowers from your yard to brighten her desk.

✻ Pray: Many teachers I know begin praying for their classes during the summer, even before they know which students they will have. Following their cue, we can start praying for our teachers-to-be even before we know who they are.

We may not know yet what our kids' teachers will do to send us into a love-struck tailspin, but we can usually be confident that our affections won't be misguided. After all, these teachers will have been hand-picked by a God who loves and cares for our kids even more than we do!

## 2. Offer a Helping Hand

Stay-at-home moms have a unique advantage of enjoying a full-time career that allows us to participate wholeheartedly in our kids' school activities. Here's a look at some ways we can help:

**TEACHER'S AID**—Most teachers, no matter how efficient, can use an extra set of hands now and again.

"I substitute in their classes when needed, drive for field trips, attend any special activities, and eat lunch with them periodically," says Tula, who knows how important it is to help her kids' teachers.

Other ways to help teachers is to let them know we're willing to spend a few hours each week doing some of the following kinds of chores:

✳ Performing "teacher's aid" stuff: grading papers, making copies, stapling pages, putting up a bulletin board ...

✳ Reading with kids who need a little one-on-one attention

✳ Reading to the class—"When Brad was in first grade," says Gina, "I started reading stories and chapter books to the class. The kids love the break from the routine, and I get such enjoyment from it!" She has continued that tradition into third grade, where she's now reading The Chronicles of Narnia every Thursday morning. A gifted storyteller, her presentation mesmerizes the kids, gives the teacher a break, provides her with a weekly peek at the class and classroom routines, and presents her a rare opportunity to minister in the public classroom through the classic C.S. Lewis allegory.

✳ Teaching the kids a hobby or skill—Spanish, papier mâché, creative writing ... teachers will love the way you can enhance their curriculum

✳ Chaperoning field trips

✳ Being a room mom who helps with parties, field trips, etc.

✳ Taking a special new pet to visit the classroom

**CAMPUS CRUSADER**—In a setting as vital and volatile as an elementary school, faculty and staff always appreciate any help a parent's willing to offer. Some things we can consider doing include:

✳ Answering the phone when the secretary's busy or out

✳ Maintaining the main bulletin board

✳ Organizing a teacher-appreciation day

✳ Pitching in on the playground patrol during recess

✳ Volunteering in the nurse's office

✳ Compiling a school newsletter

✳ Helping the librarian by offering to handle story time once a month

✳ Volunteering during special events, field trips, performances, sales, fundraisers, carnivals, etc.

## On-the-Job Hazard!

### Teacher's "Pest," Not Teacher's "Pet"

One note of caution: Since we are able to be at our child's school so much to help with various activities, it's easy to overdo it. Our desire to help can unwittingly turn into a tendency to be annoyingly intrusive. The teacher, the office staff, and the librarian have schedules that our popping in to "help" can really disrupt. The best tactics are to arrange these efforts in advance and to be respectful when our offers are not accepted.

Our efforts to donate our time, talents, and energy can yield so much. They help us establish an attitude of partnership with the school and responsibility for its operation, whether through baking a cake for a carnival or recruiting members for the parent-teacher organization. It can give us an inside track on the operation of the school, teacher personalities, routines, as well as a rare chance to see our kids in action at school—do they listen well? Are they eating dessert first and not having time to finish their sandwich? Do they cooperate on the playground? And finally, pitching in on campus helps us forge a relationship with the kids our kids spend so much time with.

## 3. Take Care of the No. 1 Customer

We may be at the school every time the doors open, our child's teacher's best and most-dependable room mom, an active force in parent-teacher organizations, and know as much about our kids' daily routines as the teachers. But to leave our kids out of the loop means none of the above will do any good.

We can help our students by:

**Helping them establish good study habits.** Set regular and reasonable homework and bedtimes, equip a kid-friendly study center, and instill some tried-and-true principles such as "don't procrastinate," "do the worst first," and "break down big jobs into more manageable pieces."

**Teaching good organizational skills.** Supply notebooks, purchase a student calendar/organizer, and post a large calendar to track upcoming due dates and tests. One mom uses dry erase board to clearly designate scheduled field trips, tests, and appointments of each family member with a different color pen for each person.

**Reading, reading, reading the info that comes home in the backpack each day.** A great habit: go through it with pen in hand and the calendar nearby because these notes, memos, and announcements are usually chock-full of coming test dates, book report dates, teacher requests, permission slips, and tests to be signed.

**Being available during homework time** to help stumped kids, to quiz kids who need to be quizzed, to derail frustration, to praise and prod studiers toward success.

**Displaying and celebrating successes and victories.** Have an "I did it" bulletin board to show off good grades, ribbons, and special projects; head for the ice cream shop to mark the meeting of a tough deadline or simply the survival of a rainy Monday when nothing seemed to go right.

**Respecting the fine lines between encouraging and nagging,** between helping and doing, and between having high expectations and setting up stressful pressure.

**Emphasizing effort as well as achievement.**

**Using failures as a challenge:** "How can we turn this around for the better?"

**Being a security net** when grades tumble and failures occur.

**Teaching study skills.** How to make study sheets, note cards, diagrams, and summaries; how to use reference tools; how to break large tasks into small ones; how to prioritize .

# Don't Leave Home without It

As moms of preschoolers, we hear lots about diaper-bag packing strategies, but it's just as important for moms of school-agers to learn how to pack a purse. Whether we're en route to the dentist, in the bleachers at a soccer game, or on a school bus with 35 second-graders heading for the museum, a well-stocked sacque can be our greatest friend.

So here goes. After picking the brains of other moms and slyly observing experienced grade-school teachers in action, here's a list of essentials for the handiest of handbags. Hint: You'd better find a roomy one to hold all this stuff!

* a reclosable bag or two (to hold the parts of a broken necklace, a pulled tooth, a soda-drenched hair bow)

* a permanent marker (for labeling drink boxes on field trips and putting names on craft projects at Scout meetings)

* safety pins (especially for recitals and programs that involve costumes)

* self-stick notes/pencil

* calendar

* sunscreen

* bobby pins

* anti-bacterial gel

* travel-size wet wipes (clean messy hands, wipe off a grungy picnic table, or soothe playground scrapes)

* tissues

* bandages

* snacks (from a pack of gum to a package of restaurant crackers, sometimes just having SOMETHING to eat can save the day)

* lip balm (to protect wind-chapped lips or to wax the string of a new yo-yo)

* small scissors

* nail file

* rubber band

* mending kit

* money (quarters are especially nice for the gum machine at the grocery store to the fish food dispenser at the zoo to the baseball field where a coach needs a coin to toss to decide who bats first)

* small toys (small fast-food-meal trinkets can help kids pass time in lines and in the car)

# Chapter 8

# your public
# relations role:
# hospitality at home

> "Offer hospitality to one another . . ." I Peter 4:9

A Midwestern mom phoned a radio program on which I was a guest; she called to voice her support of stay-at-home moms. "I've got six teen-age boys downstairs and most of their moms work," she said. "They could go to any of their empty homes after school—unsupervised—but they like to come here to hang out. They like me being here, even though I pretty much leave them alone."

She said all it usually takes to entice them to stick around is a little conversation and a batch of caramel apples from time to time.

Hospitality isn't just about lighting a couple of candles when company's coming for dinner. Although that's nice. More important, it's the perpetual motion of using our homes to serve God and all those who cross our thresholds—including muddy Boy Scout troop #42 members, the rowdy 10-year-old neighbor, and the kids—all 23—from Mr. Strommer's science class who need a place to conduct a stinky experiment.

As parents, we do these kinds of things often, without realizing the impact our gestures of hospitality can make on the young lives crisscrossing through our yard and parking for popcorn in our family room.

"It's real important for us to be hospitable to our kids' friends," says Holly Schurter, mother of eight who shares the bounty of her mothering experience through workshops. "Especially these days, I think a lot of children don't get the kind of family experiences we can offer as Christian families. We have something special in terms of how we're living—following Christ and how that changes us. A lot of kids don't get the opportunity to see that kind of love in action within a family setting."

Christ says ". . . whoever welcomes a little child like this in My name welcomes Me" (Matthew 18:5, NIV). However, although they're all "precious in His sight," as the song goes, being hospitable to kids isn't always as simple or as rewarding as showing hospitality to grown-ups. The under-12 set doesn't necessarily know how to graciously acknowledge a hostess's efforts. In fact, many moms have seen how quickly playing waitress to a ravenous pack of neighborhood playmates can leave them feeling less like the happy-go-lucky Kool-Aid moms of '70s TV commercials and more like threadbare day-care center doormats.

"When our kids were all very small, we lived in a neighborhood where there were a lot of small children," Holly recalls. "I remember one afternoon looking out into our side yard, there were 17 kids there. Our house and another house down the street were kind of the neighborhood playground.

"At times that was hard," she says. "That carries all kinds of questions like: Do you feed all those kids? Do you let them come in the house? What about when they need to go to the bathroom? Wash their hands? When they get hurt, what do you do?"

The best strategy for settling these kinds of issues and converting child-care chaos into backyard bliss is to think through possible situations and ways to handle them before they arise.

"I don't think that God requires us in every instance to give everything we have all at once," she says. That's why it's important to set some boundaries.

"Bring up those issues with your husband and talk about it, and bring it up with your kids and talk about it. Let them know what some of the issues are so they can help you. If they are helping you enforce it, it goes a lot better. But if your kids are among the ones saying, 'Gee, Mom, why can't we . . .' then you're ready to kill them!"

# Building Boundaries

As mayor of your corner of Munchkinland, you're entitled to tailor such laws and bylaws to suit your family's lifestyle. For example, a few years back, my husband and my son spent hundreds of hours and lots of dollars perfecting a miniature train set-up that eventually took over our garage. So—as enticing as it was—we had to call the system off-limits to playmates, who didn't always realize the fragility and value of the project. Maybe your kids know the riding lawnmower in the backyard is not a toy but the new kid on the block might not realize its potential danger. From "don't ride your bikes through the neighbor's yard" to "always empty your shoes before you come inside after you've been in the sandbox," clearly outline all of those kinds of rules and boundaries, and teach your children how to politely pass them on to guests. When setting playtime boundaries, consider limitations and freedoms regarding:

## TIME
My times are in Your hand.
Psalm 31:15

Do you have younger ones (or a spouse who works nights) who nap at certain times of the day? You might want to call your yard off-limits during that time span. Also think about the dinner hour. "We had a rule that when the kids came in for dinner, everybody had to go home," Holly says. That was partly for safety's sake (Mom and Dad at the dinner table means no watchful eyes on the crew outside), but she says it also encouraged playmates to go home and spend time with their own families.

## FEEDING THE MASSES

Whoever gives one of these little ones
even a cup of cold water because he is
a disciple, truly, I saw to you, he will be
no means lose his reward.   Matthew 10:42

Does that mean we feed and water each of these kids who drift through our gates day in and day out? It depends.

"You can't afford to feed them all every day," Holly notes. So she suggests two tactics: "I tried to find snacks that were nutritious and not expensive, and I tried to offer them on an irregular basis so the kids didn't know when I was going to come out with a snack or when I wasn't. I didn't want to set up an expectation."

Tidbits like crackers and peanut butter, pretzels, and fruit juices are practical. Other inexpensive snack time ideas include popcorn, inexpensive cookies such as animal crackers or vanilla wafers, Popsicles, graham crackers, Jell-O, marshmallows, dry cereal, and even just plain water. Holly says she sometimes served water with a little lemon in it and found it "surprising how kids appreciate things like that sometimes. You can also put pretzels in a little paper cup with a few raisins or something like that sprinkled in it and the kids think they've been treated so well. You can do special things to make kids feel like they're really honored guests."

Another hint: Small (bathroom-size) paper cups are great for passing out drinks, and coffee filters—especially the cone-shaped ones—make great inexpensive snack holders.

## INSIDE-OUTSIDE

"Let the little children come to Me . . .
for to such belong the kingdom of heaven."
—Matthew 19:14

Theirs may be the kingdom of heaven but we know we can't keep our homes very heavenly with kids running in and out hour after hour. The revolving-door dilemma has plagued moms since before the days of Wally and the Beav. Do you let the kids play inside? Even if you just vacuumed and mopped? Even if flies are buzzing in line to get in your kitchen? Even if you have little ones napping inside? And what is it about kids that makes them want to play outside the minute they've set up the entire Barbie household in the middle of your den floor? Think about the ins and outs of how you want to handle these scenarios.

# A LEGACY OF HOSPITALITY

As moms, showing hospitality to our kids and their friends doesn't just fulfill a biblical mandate (see 1 Peter 4:8–9 and Romans 12:13). It also teaches our children—by example, which happens to be one of the best ways they learn—how to be hospitable as well.

"If we don't offer . . . hospitality to children, how will our kids feel like they can offer hospitality as they get older?" Holly notes. "If they see it from the time that they're little on up, and we allow them to help with it and extend hospitality to their friends, it becomes a natural thing for them as they get older. They have a real deep understanding of what it costs and what it means to [be hospitable]."

With many of her kids having now reached adulthood, Holly has already been blessed with the privilege of seeing some of the fruits of her efforts throughout the years. "Now that our kids are in college, their friends still feel welcome to come and roost and visit and talk. So it's something that makes me feel good. It started back there in the yard when all these kids would come to our house."

We can teach our kids how to be hospitable not only by our example, but by getting them involved in preparations for guests. One secret of being a hostess at-the-ready, Holly says, is to keep at least one area of the house constantly cleared away for the possible drop-in. In some homes, it might be the formal living room, in others, a couple of nice chairs in a cozy corner of the den might be off-limits to clutter. Recruit the kids' cooperation in keeping these areas junk free by letting them use the space for their guests as well. That way, Holly says, "they get a feeling for why that space is important."

To be further prepared for unexpected visitors, try to keep something special in the pantry or freezer off-limits until the need arises. Because a nice tin of cookies tucked away in a remote corner can be a mighty strong temptation for hungry tykes, rally the troops' cooperation by letting them know that those cookies are reserved for special guests.

Another way to encourage our kids in the art of hospitality is to lead them through a series of what-if scenarios. "A lot of times we expect our kids to be hospitable, but we don't show them how," Holly says.

"When we knew we were having company, I would let the kids help me get ready. I began role-playing with them while we would do the work. I would say, 'Okay, somebody's at the door. It's Aunt Grizelda. How are you going to introduce her to somebody?' Then when those situations would come up, they had already tried it with me. They were more comfortable doing it with guests because they had practiced it with me. It's not a guarantee that our kids will be perfectly well-mannered all the time, but it certainly increases the odds."

# OPENING YOUR HEART TO OTHERS

## (OR DON'T LET YUCKY CARPET INHIBIT YOUR INNER HOSTESS)

I'm not proud to admit that my hospitality history bears the scars of many missed opportunities. A baby shower I didn't offer to give because we had buckling brown carpet. A Sunday school fellowship I refrained from hosting because I didn't think we had enough room. A Christmas brunch I decided against planning because I didn't believe I could afford all the trimmings that would make it special enough to take my friends away from their other activities.

But Holly points out that hospitality is not about me, my ugly carpet, my small living room, or the mismatched glasses lurking in my cabinets. It's about keeping my heart, not my home, ready to minister to my guest's needs.

"In my case, we had so many small children, our

house was never clean," Holly says. "But did God me to be Martha Stewart? Obviously not. He called me to be who I am here in this place, under these circumstances."

So she adopted a gracious attitude that says: "This is the best I have to offer today. I'll clear the laundry off and I'll put it in a basket and ask, 'Would you like a cup of tea?' when guests pop by.

"That way, the focus is not on me, or what I have. The focus is on you. You're my guest. God has allowed you come to my door.

"Our kids need to learn that you want to honor your guests by offering the best you have, and that means you want to keep things picked up as much as possible. But realistically, that's not always going to be what the house looks like when people come. So get your mind off yourself and what's wrong with you and put your mind on the other person and why God has led them to you."

Hmmmm, after hearing Holly's take on hospitality, I think I'll invite some friends and their kids over for dinner Friday night. . . .

Chapter 9

# your job
# as social secretary:
# how much is too much?

. . . the LORD will watch over your
coming and going both now and
forevermore. Psalm 121:8, NIV

We're all familiar with the stereotypical
hurried kid, whose usual afternoon and
evening includes changing from school
clothes to a gymnastics leotard in the back
seat of the car as Mom scouts out the nearest
fast-food outlet to pick up an energy-boosting
supper of fries and soft drink between stops.
After gymnastics, it's over to a friend's house
to carpool to art lessons, and only after that
does the pooped 8-year-old get to come
home, kick off her shoes and wiggle her bare
toes in the carpet before plopping on the

couch for some down time with her favorite show. But wait! "Get into your uniform! You've got a game tonight," Mom shouts to her brother, that hysterical edge in her voice as she digs through the hamper to find the socks she hasn't had time to wash since the last game. The girl and her brother grab tacos from the take-out sack on the breakfast bar and shovel them down as they jump into the back seat.

This snapshot of childhood isn't one any of us would want to paste into our kids' memory books. But at least parts of this scenario are all too familiar in many of our own homes. When the kids hit grade-school age, it seems, the opportunities for lessons and organized extracurricular activities start knocking at our door, and like the battery bunny, they just keep on knocking and knocking and knocking. We begin to feel more like chauffeurs than mothers.

It's easy to let our kids' involvement snowball, I think, because really, there's nothing wrong with lessons and activities. In fact, there's a lot that's right about them. For example, "They provide good learning experiences and build confidence," notes DeAnn, mom of two. This kind of activity can also help kids tap into their talents and strengths.

"I want to expose [my son] to a variety of things so he can decide what he really likes, and hopefully narrow down the field," explains Gina.

Tula says this is her motive for allowing her kids to participate in organized activities as well. "We have tried to discover each child's special gifts and point them in that direction," she says. "For example, my oldest daughter excels in drama so we have her in piano and drama activities at church. My middle child is extremely gifted in dance, so she works with a young lady in our church 30 minutes a week. My son is very athletic. He plays baseball in the summer and basketball in the fall."

Participation in sports and activities also offers much-needed physical activity in this sedentary society and can also offer important lessons about self-discipline and dependability, teamwork, and cooperation. They can place children in a new circle of friends with the same interests. "Since my kids are home-schooled, they need the contact with other children," notes Mary, mom of two.

# COMMIT TO STOP OVERCOMMITTING

With all the plusses of getting our kids involved in a variety of activities, how do we go wrong when we sign the permission slip for Tae Kwon Do, piano lessons, or the bike club? It boils down to one word: overcommitment. Moms who have it all together stress that this is something they must consciously avoid.

"There are just not enough hours in the day to accomplish all that needs to be done, much less all we want to do," says Gina. "Even Bradley has expressed frustration over not enough time to just be together as a family and do nothing. So for sanity—not to mention financial drain—we limit our activities." Right now, she says, what's working for Bradley is involvement in Boy Scouts and one sport per season, except during summer, which "we leave open for family activities."

When considering what to let your kids join, it's helpful to ask the following questions before making your decision:

## 1. Why?
### Give serious thought as to why you're giving this activity serious thought.

"Everything is so competitive," says author and mom Sharon Hoffman. "Kids are being forced to grow up and forced to mature so quickly and they're put into that hectic pace so quickly that they're not even having a childhood. We need to ask, 'Is this going to matter two years from now?' Or 'Is this going to matter in light of eternity?'"

Does the activity you're considering reflect a real passion of your child or does it represent your own wishes for your child? Just because you grew up on the softball field doesn't mean your daughter will be as well suited for the sport. She may prefer canvas and paint-brush to cleats and balls.

## 2. Is it a good fit?

Make sure the activity suits your child's personality. Some kids prefer the independence of sports and activities such as tennis and art, while others thrive on the teamwork and interaction of ball teams and service organizations. Some kids seem to embrace and enjoy competition; others shy away from competitive activity, instead deriving their best dose of confidence from personal achievements such as a completed painting or an expertise in rock collecting.

## 3. Is my son or daughter ready for this?

Make sure your child is ready to make the commitment. Just because organized sports and lessons are offered in your community for kids as young as three, don't rush them into anything. Starting a four-year-old in tee-ball when his stage of development is telling you he'd rather watch bugs in the grass than field grounders is only likely to cause "baseball burnout" by the time he's eight or nine.

## 4. How much time will it take?

Research the time investment. The time required to participate in some organized sports and activities can be deceptive. Find out all you can about requirements beyond meetings, practices and games. For example, Lindsey's soccer team practiced once a week and played one game a week for two months each spring. So it was a fairly straightforward schedule easily managed. Baseball, on the other hand, was much more involved. Practices and games usually claimed Nick two or three times a week, sometimes more. In addition, baseball parents committed to a once-a-season, daylong turn at the concession stand and to help during a late spring car wash fundraiser. Further, baseball isn't limited to the regular season schedule. There are pre-season and post-season tournaments, all-star teams, fall leagues, etc., that can stretch an expected spring and early summer commitment into a nearly year-round affair.

"Tyler played baseball last year at age seven from March until November," says Tonya. Making it to the total of more than seventy games during that stretch really slammed a fist into her family's together time, and the whole episode taught them a valuable lesson: "It taught us to guard our down time to be at home together as a family instead of being at the ball park every night," she says. "Tyler agreed!"

Other organized activities such as service organizations and clubs often involve regular meetings as well as special events like parades, service/community projects, banquets, and ceremonies. These extras take chunks of time outside of meeting time to plan, prepare, and attend. Lessons such as dance and gymnastics may call for weekly instruction time on top of additional rehearsals as recitals and programs draw near. Often, these programs fall late in the spring, just in time for final tests and major

project due dates. The message here is to go into an activity with your eyes wide open. Don't just ask teachers, coaches, instructors for a run-down of the time commitment; it's their main focus and what you consider to be a large quantity of time may not be seem like enough to them. A better bet is to ask parents and kids who have been involved in the programs you're considering.

## 5. How much will it cost?

There's no way to prepare parents for the onslaught of "pay for thises" and "buy me thats" that raising school-age kids brings. From growing through two shoe sizes each semester to needing cavities filled and braces installed, sometimes it's almost all we parents in one-income families can do to keep up with even the basic upkeep of our kids. So when the sign-up sheets start to circulate, we shouldn't feel Scroogish as we closely analyze the merits of each activity to decide how to best spend our budgeted activity and organization dollars.

To get a clear reading of your investment, always ask up front what's required: Tuition? Deposit? Uniform? Supply and equipment fees? Beyond that, find out specifically what your dollars will pay for: Art supplies? Hat and jersey? What supplies or equipment are you expected to buy on your own? Find out when and how you are expected to pay. Monthly? Yearly? Per lesson? Do you pay for missed lessons? Is there an opportunity to make up missed lessons? Down the road, will there be tournament fees or lodging expenses for away games? What about ballpark admission—do parents and siblings pay to see each game? How much will recital costumes run? What about other incidentals that may throw inadvertent blows to your budget—take-out food each Thursday because that's meeting night; concession stand cash, etc. What about the ongoing costs of this new skill or hobby? For example, if your son takes tennis, is there a public tennis court nearby where he can fine-tune his training? Or will you have to pay a private facility to use the courts each time he wants to play? Finding out specifics now can help you avoid having to head to the bench before the game's over.

## 6. How will this activity fit into the rest of our schedule?

This activity won't be an isolated event in the life of your family. Find out what will need to be the game plan if you commit to this activity. For example, when are the lessons or practices held? Do they encroach on church or other family commitments? Do they overlap or bump uncomfortably against other commitments? The obligations may fit neatly into your calendar: 3:30 den meeting, 4:30 dance, 6:00 ball practice. But in reality those commitments don't fit all that neatly when you consider key details like kids need to use the bathroom and have a snack right after school, they need time to change clothes, and they need a decent supper and adequate rest. Allow for those needs. When the puzzle pieces overlap instead of fitting together, just say no. You can rest assured, another opportunity will come along sooner or later that will be a better fit.

## 7. Does it feel right?

Vague, I know. But it's important to get a feel for the

environment of the activity or organization you're considering. But try to find out the underlying philosophy of each activity you're considering. If it's a competitive sport, cue in on whether you sense a philosophy of "we want to win at any cost" or of the more upbeat attitude of "we're a team and we'll do our best." Do the coaches seem demanding and argumentative or patient and encouraging? Does the service group involve a group of kids and parents who really stress teamwork and service or do they seem more concerned with getting their picture in the local paper for the deeds they do?

# SPORTS SENSE

The first time I sat through a dismal ball game holding a flattened popcorn box over my head to keep the rain from dribbling into my eyes, I knew I had a lot to learn about being an effective sports mom.

But Amanda, mother of four (ages seven, five, two, and three months) whose first foray into sports was a season of tee-ball last year, seems to have it all together concerning the bleacher scene. "With a little planning, we as parents can be comfortable in any condition," she says. She recommends sports families pack the following items in what she calls a "Little League Survival Kit." A duffle or gym bag is perfect, she says, adding that parents should keep it at-the-ready in the closet or car trunk.

"Obviously some of these items will have to be replenished after each game," she says, "but you get the idea. You can make baseball, or any other sport, an enjoyable experience for your child and the whole family." I have only a couple more things to add to Amanda's list: a towel (to sit on, wipe off wet bleachers, dry off wet kids, or swab off muddy cleats) and . . . an umbrella!

---

Little League Survival Kit: Do you have?

○ **Blanket** ○ Sunglasses ○ **Baseball cap (of course!)**
○ Extra hair tie for each girl in the family cheering section
○ **Sunscreen** ○ Lip balm ○ **Kleenex** ○ Water bottle
○ **Bag of chips or popcorn or granola bars**
○ Light jacket ○ **Small bag for garbage (plastic grocery bags work great)** ○ Small toy(s) for younger children ○ **Small stamps and ink pad and paper**
○ Box of crayons and coloring book

# part three

# what about me?

There are no magic formulas to help us gain our equilibrium between the ups and downs this child-centered life places in front of us. But there are some ways to find balance and, yes, good health in body, mind and spirit.

# Chapter 10

# your health package: body, mind and soul

> He gently leads those that have young. Isaiah 40:11

When you go for a job interview in the workforce, often one of the first questions you have about your prospective employer may be what health benefits are offered. Most employers want to provide their staff with a good health insurance package because they know healthy employees are productive employees.

While I have yet to find a stay-at-home-parent policy, the same principle applies to we how work at home. Healthy parents are indeed productive and effective parents. But what makes us healthy? At times, because of the unique demands of our job, we may seem far from a picture of health, whether we're talking about our physical, mental or spiritual condition. When you venture beyond the procedures manual of stay-at-home mothering, you'll wander into the hearts of women at home. There you may find us precariously perched on life's teeter-totter between exasperation and exhilaration; you'll find us indignantly defending our decision to stay at home one minute and nervously wondering what we've done with our lives the next.

There are no magic formulas to help us gain our equilibrium between the ups and downs this child-centered life places in front of us. But there are some ways to find balance—and, yes, good health—in body, mind and spirit.

# LET'S GET PHYSICAL

When was the last time you had seven or eight hours of sleep, three well-balanced meals, and a brisk walk around the block—all within one 24-hour chunk of time? Sounds simple enough, but with a busy family in the house, it's not an easy thing to do. Here's some tried and true advice for keeping physically fit.

**GET PLENTY OF REST.** If you have an infant at home, try to sleep whenever the baby does. Active kids can go seemingly forever without sleep. Their parents can't. If you have an older child, insist on a rest period or quiet time to give each of you a break. And if that doesn't help much, try to get into bed a little earlier, sleep a little later, or cut back on commitments to conserve energy.

**EAT RIGHT.** Some of us, since we're at home and have access to the pantry and fridge all day long, nibble nonstop, which isn't good. And others of us, since we're so busy corralling kids, don't even remember to eat a bite until we're feeling light-headed and dizzy. Then we look at the clock, see that it's 2 P.M., and realize that all we've had all day is a couple of soft drinks and some animal cookies. That's not good either. This may sound trite, but be sure to eat right so you'll have energy, be resistant to those annoying viruses the kids pick up, and enjoy better health all around.

**EXERCISE REGULARLY.** Aerobics, fitness programs, jogging, walking—the list of physical fitness options is endless, so you don't have much of an excuse for not working some kind of exercise into your day. If the kids are an obstacle to your exercise regime, incorporate them into it. Put on some bouncy music and get everyone in on the action!

**PUT YOUR BEST FACE FORWARD.** Most moms who stay at home have learned that keeping up their physical appearance helps them feel better and stay at least a few steps ahead in the self-esteem game.

"When you leave the workforce, your attitude about yourself changes," says Karen after her third year at home with her three boys. "You go from wearing business suits to blue jeans or sweats every day. Some days you have a hard time getting out of bed, let alone putting on makeup and fixing your hair. 'Why should I do that? I'm going to be here with the babies all day. No one's going to see me, so why bother?' But if I don't go ahead and go through the process of trying to make myself presentable, it changes my whole attitude."

"I try to avoid feeling down about myself because once I get down, it's hard to get out of that feeling," says Laurie. "I make sure I at least brush my hair, brush my teeth, and get dressed every day. Also, I try to put on makeup. I've found that looking good makes me feel much better about myself."

Saying you're going to look your best most of the time is one thing but doing it is another when little ones are around and when your budget's lean. For one thing, with all the new priorities kids bring into the picture, you may not have much time to spend in front of the mirror. And for another, even if you can make the time, it can be hard to physically get that makeup on with a far-reaching baby on one hip. But take heart—putting your best face forward shouldn't take more time each morning than you can realistically spare.

✳ **Keep baby entertained** by stowing a box or basket filled with child-proof "beauty" toys under your bathroom cabinet. Empty shampoo bottles, plastic soap dishes, a rinsed-out hairspray bottle filled with water, hair curlers, a soft brush and comb, an unbreakable mirror, a sea sponge, an empty tissue box, play jewelry, and a pretend shave kit will keep your little one busy while you get your face fixed— right down to your mascara, without one smudge.

✳ **Rethink your beauty regimen.** Can you simplify it in any way?

✳ **Consider a different haircut**, one that would keep you from having to spend time blow-drying or curling it each morning.

✳ Instead of trying to get in and out of the shower as quickly as you can each morning, **consider switching to relaxing baths** every evening after baby's gone to bed.

✳ **Clean out that makeup drawer or shelf.** Throw away old makeup and lotions. This will save you the time it takes to rummage through the drawer to find what you need each morning. Better yet, get your makeup out of that drawer and into a counter-top organizer that lets you see everything at a glance.

✳ **Straighten that closet.** Forget what the fashion experts say about grouping skirts, jackets, pants, shirts, etc., together on the rod. You don't have time to create a new look each morning as you hunt for a blouse to creatively coordinate with some pants you've pulled out. Hang your pieces that go together

together! You'll be ready in a flash and you won't waste time trying to decide whether that jacket looks good with that skirt.

✴ **Put socks in a see-through plastic box** so you can get your hands on the right ones right away.

✴ **Hang scarves, belts, and other accessories in plain view** on a rack or hanger so you can spot what you need in the blink of an eye.

✴ When you do shop for yourself (a foreign concept to many stay-at-home moms!), **don't give up your style,** just alter it to suit your new career. If you love dresses, stay away from the dry-clean-only ones you bought for the office and pick up some washable, no-iron ones you can wear with comfy flats or strappy sandals to the park, the pediatrician's office, a room-mothers meeting, or lunch with a pal.

✴ **Pay attention to details.** Take that extra minute each morning to put on those earrings. Invest in a good purse that looks great with all your clothes. Purchase socks to match your outfits. Going the extra mile can make the difference between looking and feeling half-done and looking and feeling confident. Remember our Proverbs friend who "smiles at the future." In addition to describing this woman's faith in her Creator, doesn't that spell head-held-high confidence in the life He gave you?

# MINDING THE MIND

It's easy to get so busy being moms that we forget to keep ourselves mentally and emotionally charged up.

# On-the-Job Hazard!

## Fumbling Fashion

We may not get out very often; we may have a limited budget; we may just be cold. For a number of seemingly excellent reasons we tend to pull on sweatshirts or other scruffy clothes when we know we'll just be home with the kids. Then we wonder why our self-esteem plunges when a friend drops by or when we run into a group of spiffy-looking room moms during a quick run to the school to deliver a forgotten lunch. Let's make a deal: Let's each just pick up one pair of sweats for painting projects or for snow days and spend the rest of our clothes budget on go-anywhere, easy-care knits and denims. We'll be just as comfy and we'll look a lot more together, which in turn will make us feel more together.

Karen, mother of two, admits that not getting enough mental exercise was one of her biggest fears going into stay-at-home motherhood. "I feared not being intellectually stimulated," said the former college instructor who holds an advanced degree in the sciences. She found that homeschooling her children has made the mental challenges "real, daily and interesting."

Here are some other ways to keep our mind—and emotions—in tact amid the demands of child-rearing.

**Find or make personal time** to relax, read a book, shop, enjoy a hobby, have lunch with a friend, pray.

**Nurture existing friendships** and cultivate new ones.

**Get out of the house.** "Being the only stay-at-home mom in my church," says Laurie, "I must go outside my church family to find friends to keep me from feeling shut up and alone at home. I am involved in a Bible study, MOPS, and an aerobics class. I've found I must make myself get out of the house. It's a lot of trouble to get myself and my child fed, dressed, and get our things together, but once we get out, I feel great."

**Be yourself.** Don't try to be what everybody else thinks a stay-at-home mom should be. Develop your own style, establish your own routines. Let your lifestyle reflect your personality. You're no longer in the workplace where you have to follow someone else's time clock, someone else's rules. Set your own agenda and enjoy the freedom! If you like music, turn it on and turn it up during the day. The kids probably won't complain. If you enjoy needlepoint, let the dishes go for a little while and get a good start on that next project. I'm not endorsing irresponsibility; I'm encouraging enjoying life and celebrating your God-given talents and desires. See Ecclesiastes 5:18.

**Avoid comparisons.** I know I've had a great day if I've managed to make the beds, unload the dishwasher, teach Erin the difference between inside voice and outside voice, run a couple of errands, help Lindsey and Nick with homework, and have clean stacks of laundry resting like trophies on our bed by the time Kurt's due home in the evening. On days when I've accomplished this much, I'm walking pretty tall.

Until a friend calls. She has meandered to the subject of laundry and casually mentions that she always makes sure her laundry's put away before her husband gets home. I feel my sense of accomplishment melting away like a Popsicle on the patio. By the time my husband walks in the front door, I'm frantically throwing clothes in drawers and towels in cabinets, feeling desperate and defensive. Because I'm figuring if I was half the woman my friend is, I would have gotten out of bed half an hour earlier just to make sure the laundry was put away before the little hand got to the six and the big hand got to the 12. But that attitude's no good. If I continually use my friends' performances as the yardstick by which I assess my success, I will never measure up. God's advice is always good advice: "But let each one test his own work, and then his reason to boast will be in himself alone and not in his neighbor. For each will have to bear his own load" (Galatians 6:4–5).

**Fight off the supermom syndrome.** The mindset that makes you think you can bring home the bacon and fry it up in the pan, that you should be all things to all people, always producing nothing but perfect results in your every endeavor isn't reserved for working moms. Some of us who gave up the fast track pursue full-time parenting with the same competitive spirit cultivated in the business world. We may believe full-time mothering should guarantee that we will produce perfect kids. Or, more often, we begin to believe that since we don't work, we should not only join but run the school's parent volunteer organization, pitch in at the homeless shelter and the March of Dimes, sit on three church committees and direct the nursery, lead a Scout troop, baby-sit our working neighbor's kids, hand-craft all our Christmas presents, grow our own vegetables, and design and stencil all our gift-wrap.

"I guess I really thought I would be supermom to the extent that I could do everything," says Karen. Because of the isolation she felt after making the jump from a busy job where she had cultivated a circle of friends to staying at home where she had virtually no friends, she found it hard in the beginning to say no to demands on her time.

"I'd be so tired that I would not be of any use to my kids, my husband, or anybody. You have to know where to draw the line. You have to just do what you can do, and then stop."

"It's hard keeping everyone happy at the same time: my kids, my husband, my parents, my friends," says Robin, mother of two. "Since I'm at home, everybody thinks I can do all their running around."

Handling this issue might be one of the most difficult problems moms at home face because our self-esteem is so often entangled in the issue of what we do as opposed to who we are. No easy formula can help you determine how many morsels of activity your plate can adequately hold. Use the God-given gift of common sense when deciding how much you can handle. If you find yourself overloaded, make yourself say, "I can't do this project anymore. It's taking too much time away from my family."

Chere, mother of five who has been at home since her first son was born 19 years ago, says, "I have learned to say no to anything that is going to take time away from my family at this point in my life. I used to feel guilty for not doing more at my church . . . but I've realized in the past few years that I can't do it all and right now my responsibility is to my family."

This discerning mom realizes that God doesn't tell us we should do everything or be everything; we heap this kind of pressure on ourselves. All He requires of us is that we 'do justice, love kindness, and walk humbly with Him' (Micah 6:8 ). Any activities we take on that compromise our ability to follow that heavenly guidance just aren't worth it and, frankly, makes us run the risk of placing our own expectations ahead of God.

"I am truly trying to find the balance in an active home," says Leslie, a seasoned stay-at-home mother of five. "I believe it is wise to redeem our time in a way that truly honors the Lord and our families," she says. "It takes much prayer to find the balance between what is good to do and what are the best things to do."

So when supermom syndrome threatens, remember that we aren't perfect; only Jesus was perfect. Only Jesus could handle all the world and Satan threw at Him. We, on the other hand, need to cut ourselves some slack and rely on the forgiveness He offers.

**STAY IN TOUCH.** Since I quit my job to stay at home with the kids, I've been afraid I'll do something out in public that will label me as being out of touch. You know, like actress Terri Garr did in the movie Mr. Mom: She reached across the table and began to neatly cut her new boss's steak into small pieces for him. It's easy to be a little out of touch when we're mothering young kids at home. We may not get out as often; we may not socialize as much; more days than not we may not even get the chance to read the newspaper or watch the evening news. Sometimes just remembering what day it is poses a monumental challenge.

But for your own self-esteem and for the benefit of your family and friends, stay plugged into the real world. Read books (try something other than parenting and child development books), spend time with friends, watch the news, read the newspaper, take a college course, learn a new skill, or volunteer in an organization whose ideals you embrace, go to church to remain connected with your church family.

## PUTTING DREAMS ON HOLD

Deciding to stay at home full-time often can derail a woman's plans and dreams. For example, the limited funds of operating a home on one income may prohibit a woman from pursuing her dream of finishing college. And the time-consuming demands of caring for a growing family may leave no spare minutes for another to dabble in the arts and crafts hobby she loves. But putting such dreams on hold doesn't mean having to hit the delete button altogether, Sharon Hoffman, author of *Come Home to Comfort*, points out. As we read in Ecclesiastes 3:1, "there is a season, and a time for every matter under heaven," but that doesn't mean there's time for us to do everything under heaven all at once! Here is Sharon's story:

"There are some things I put way on the back burner for 21 years, basically, because I knew I did not have the emotional energy and time since I was raising two daughters in the vocation the Lord called me to," says Sharon. "A lot of the things I put off were desires of my heart that I knew I would not just want to let go of. I wrote one book before my second child was born and I began to see that [my writing] was not going to continue while raising two young daughters.

"I found that I was a growly mom, I was not reasonable, I was crabby and uptight all the time when I was trying to do everything and nothing was ending up being done well.

"I made a conscious choice at that time that I cannot be good at everything. If I was going to be a good writer, then I would have write; if I was going to be a good mom and wife, then I would have to be a good mom and wife."

So Sharon decided to put down her proverbial pen to devote her all to her daughters.

"It was kind of letting go of a dream—but really it was deferring a dream. I always hoped I would get the opportunity to write again. And I knew if it was of God, then I would.

"When I just focused on the two or three things that, at that stage of my life, I knew were the best things for me to do, then I felt like I gave it my all. I did my very best at those things."

Once her girls left home to forge lives of their own, Sharon says the years she had given up for them didn't seem like they had been long at all. In fact, "they seemed like just a blink away." And the dedicated mom's writing aspirations, as it turns out, never boiled dry. In fact, "The very fall that both of our girls went to college . . . I began to respond to the yearning to write that I didn't even remember had been there all along." Once she picked up pen again, she found two exciting results:

"I was able to be very good at it because it was my major priority of thought, and it also gave me a sense that I'm not going through a morbid stage of my life because my girls are grown. Rather, it opened up doors to a new exciting phase of my life. I could never be traveling like I do if I had a family at home and I could never close myself in my office and set office hours if I had kids in the home.

"It's been a real wonderful, poignant lesson for me to remember when I have other dreams I'm wanting to fulfill and am not able to at this time in my life. I remember that what I'm doing right now was on the back burner for years, too. So someday I'll get to do those other neat things.

"Moms need to hear that, to let the fire still be on low but to remember that no one else can raise those children."

# NOURISHING THE SPIRIT

It's easy to let spiritual needs go unattended because they are intangible and can seem very impractical in light of the 17 other things we need to be doing at the moment. But I don't have to tell you that if you let this area of your life go untended, everything else can go haywire in a heartbeat. Here are some ideas to help you stay on your toes, spiritually speaking.

Make quiet time/prayer time/Bible study a priority. I was in a MOPS Bible study group with one mom who said she set her alarm clock for 4:30 a.m. each day just so she'd have some quiet time to have a cup of coffee solo and to read her daily devotion. We moms give and give so much; we've got to make sure we get replenished. Time spent in quiet communion with the Lord is the perfect way to do this—whether it's at 4:30 a.m. or 11 p.m. or somewhere between. One morning when I was feeling particularly stressed over typical mothering problems, I grabbed some quiet time and decided to delve into a chapter of the Bible I had never studied before. I turned to the book of Ecclesiastes, not knowing much about it other than its tranquil tone and the "to everything there is a season" passage. But once I started reading through the chapters, I just knew that God had designed them just for moms like me who sometimes feel overwhelmed. Here is a brief look at the lessons I learned:

---

### There is nothing new under the sun.
### (Ecclesiastes 1:9)

How comforting to know that moms all the way back to Eve have gone through all the stuff we go through each day, both big and small. Children through the ages have had runny noses, the chicken pox, and worse. They've always teethed, been picked on by other children, swallowed things they shouldn't, been rebellious, accidentally broken a neighbor's something-or-other, gotten in trouble at school. Eve could give a heart-rending account of her firsthand experience with sibling rivalry and the loss of a child; Jochebed could describe feeling nearly paralyzed with fear for her son, Moses; and wouldn't it be grand to talk with Mary about both the worries and the wonders of pregnancy—an unexpected one at that! So if you're feeling like you don't know how to handle whatever it is you're going through with your own kids, turn to Scripture and take comfort in the fact that you're not the first! Just as God worked all things to His good for the mothers in the Bible, He will work all things for our good in His time.

## It's not always about good things.
### (Ecclesiastes 2:4–11)

Martha Stewart's trademark comment, "it's a good thing," has echoed through thousands of living rooms as many a mom watched television to derive domestic inspiration. Lots of times, as full-time moms, we try to order our world to create a paradise within the walls of our homes. We think that making our own jellies, decorating our own gift-wrap, growing our own herbs, or throwing the perfect party can be our ticket to Martha's appealing brand of paradise. While none of these actions, in and of themselves, are bad, Ecclesiastes 2 gently points out that nothing we can do can give us peace. Only a day-by-day, minute-by-minute connection with our heavenly Designer can position us to receive our portion of peace on earth and secure our lavishly decorated room in the heavenly mansion He's lovingly preparing for us even as we speak.

## There's a time for everything.
### (Ecclesiastes 3:1–8)

As moms, it's our time to do lots of things—and in a relatively short amount of time. That calls for us to become experts in time management and masters at the art of prioritizing. So when you're feeling like you're floundering and you just don't know how to order your to do list as you try to juggle the kids, your marriage, housework, volunteer work, etc., read Ecclesiastes 3 for a medicinal meditation that will give you a sense of life's rhythm and help you develop some balance. Ecclesiastes 3 tells me this is my time for planting the Word of God into my young ones' hearts, morals into their character, and a sense of order and security into their lives (verse 2); building my marriage, my family and my home on the foundation of His Word (verse 3); laughing at the antics of my kids and at the hilarity of the crazy situations parenting places me in; dancing to lullabies with a my swaddled baby or in the bleachers when my son kicks a winning soccer goal; embracing my upset toddler, my tired husband or my homework-weary teen; mending hurt feelings, skinned knees or torn blue jeans; being silent—whether tiptoeing out of the bedroom of a sleeping child or keeping my mouth shut when one of my children is about to do something her own way, which happens to be the sure-fail way; and for loving (verse 8), another word for parenting.

## We have a heart full of eternity.
## (Ecclesiastes 3:11)

"I'm having one of those days." We've all said that from time to time. Sick kids, broken down cars, a negative checking account balance, dismal weather, appliance malfunctions, doubts about giving up career for home, sibling rivalry that reaches an all-time ferocity. These yucky days are the days that it's easy to lose focus and wish away time by launching into countdowns. "When we get more money . . . " "When the kids get bigger . . . " "When ball season is over . . . " But "one of our biggest joy stealers is wishing for that next stage of life when we can enjoy the moment," says Sharon Hoffman, author of *Come Home to Comfort.* "We just need to slow down and enjoy the stage of life that we're at right now because it's not going to last forever. At any age that our children are in, we need to live for the moment. The day's going to come when someday you'll wish you had one day of that." This kind of advice helps snap me back into focus when I'm having one of those days. It opens my ears to really hear Lindsey when she sings "God wants me for a sunbeam" to her dolls in her room; to delight, not despair, when she and Nick quarrel over who gets to say the dinner prayer; and to notice that Nick's just given Lindsey one of his dollars so she can buy the notebook she wants. Then I realize I am so thankful to be able to be at home, where I get a minute-by-minute chance to tackle challenges with eternal significance. Solomon said that God has set eternity in our hearts (Ecclesiastes 3:11) . . . what big cargo for such a humble little boat as me. I have the privilege of not only being able to walk with Christ in my own life so I can tap into that eternity, but also to become the God-designed tugboat He can use to draw my own precious little ones into His kingdom!

## Two are better than one.
### (Ecclesiastes 4:9–12)

If you're feeling isolated in your at-home career—if you feel the only places you ever see are your home, the church and the school—seek a partner. Naturally husbands are pretty terrific partners in parenting. But it's still important to find another friend, better yet, several friends, who can help you pick your way through the obstacle course of parenting. My closest friend has children about the same ages as mine and I wouldn't take a room full of chocolate—no, make that a house full of Cadbury creme-filled eggs—for the encouragement she's given me as I whine to her about my busy calendar, my contrary offspring, my day-long morning sickness, my insecurities—no, my panic attacks—about new projects I've taken on. If you don't have many friends, begin praying today that God will lead you to someone who can fill that role and to whom you, in turn, can minister to as well.

---

## You can't take it with you.
### (Ecclesiastes 4:15)

If you are having doubts as to whether you should remain at home because it seems just too tough to make ends meet on one income, remember that God has so much to say about the insignificance of wealth and at every turn He promises to provide for our every need. Rather than ask, "Can we afford to keep sacrificing one income in order for me to stay at home?" ask yourself, "How can we afford for me not to make our family and kids a priority?" It's not easy to pinch pennies day in and day out, especially in this society that tells us to spend, spend, spend. But it does get easier with practice and perseverance! "Better one handful with tranquility than two handfuls with toil and chasing after the wind." Remember—that tranquility comes from God alone, not for our efforts, our riches, our status, or our "things."

---

## These are the days!
### (Ecclesiastes 9:7)

Mothering is a stressful job. There's just no way

around it. It's physically demanding and it takes us on a roller coaster of emotions. The kicker is that while we're doing it, we're expected to carry out an endless number of additional vocations: Wife, daughter, friend, church member, soccer coach, parent-teacher volunteer, informed citizen, cautious consumer. When all that leaves you feeling overwhelmed, just take a few minutes and meditate on this verse. It's a love letter from God: "Go, eat your food with gladness, and drink your wine with a joyful heart, for it is NOW [emphasis mine] that God favors what you do" (Ecclesiastes. 9:7 NIV).

See what "ecclesiastical encouragement" I found during one of my morning walks with the Lord? I challenge you to try it—you'll soon be looking forward to the encouragement He has waiting for you in His Word each day. Now back to some more ways to stay spiritually charged up:

**KEEP A JOURNAL.** The months and years spent parenting young children at home can include some of the most extreme, exhausting, and exhilarating moments imaginable. You won't want to forget them!

During my one-in-the-buggy and one-on-the-hip days, I often would not get one bed made or more than a couple household chores scratched off my todo list. Even now, with all three well past that stage, I am still surprised at how nonstop demanding these angels of mine can be. Through it all, however, I have sporadically managed to keep a journal. Although I am a writer, I don't keep a journal as a literary endeavor with any particular commercial or sentimental end in sight. I keep it because the pace of my life is so frenzied, so scattered, that I hope it might help me keep track of these days so I can go back later and sort it all out, see some details I might have missed, and remember some of the things I've forgotten.

It is both a joy and a privilege to raise infants, toddlers, preschoolers, kids at home without the added pressures and distractions of a full-time career outside the home. I know I will always want to remember what it feels like. But I also know I never will be able to recapture the true sense of the days unless I write some of it down. Time is flying at a pace well out of my control, and my journal slows the hands of the clock. Keeping it gives me comfort because no matter what crazy circumstances derail the course of my day, I will have recorded in the loopy and irregular penmanship of my own hand tidbits of information about our lives that I can later, when the kids are less demanding and are out of my immediate periphery, retrieve. I can turn one of those baby-days vignettes over and over in my head as a child turns over a beautiful stone in his hand, inspecting each angle, feeling the smooth hollow of one side and the abrasive ridges of another.

Another great thing about journals is this: In the working world, you may have had job performance reviews that gave you a chance to look back and see what you had accomplished and to help you plan where you needed to be going. A personal journal can serve a similar purpose. If you'll take a few minutes every day or couple of days to note significant (and insignificant) events in your kids' lives, prayers you've offered, and what's on your heart, you can look back, celebrate accomplishments, praise God for answered prayers, and reap the rewards of spiritual growth. I keep two journals: The first I keep for my children, where I record information with much more heart than the blanks in their baby books allow. The second is my personal journal, meant for my eyes only, in which I have recorded the best and worst days of my life, prayers, thoughts about Scripture, my struggles with the downside of at-home mothering, and my praise and thanksgiving during its victories.

**QUENCH BURNOUT.** Moms in both single- and dual-career families wonder whether they've got enough reserve fuel in their tanks to keep giving and giving and giving the way "good" moms and wives are supposed to.

"It is a 24-hour a day job," points out Shari. "You don't get many breaks, and you're always needed. It takes a lot of energy, creativity, and commitment."

For one thing, there are the physical demands. Nursing infants wake up every 45 minutes. Rambunctious toddlers crawl under and climb up anything. Rowdy kindergartners might explode before your eyes unless you take them to the park to burn off some of that simmering energy.

Every day you carry them, hoist them in and out of the bathtub, push them in their strollers, pull them in their wagons, cradle them in your arms, rock them, change their diapers, run potty-trainees to the bathroom, play catch with them, chase lightning bugs with them, tickle them, wrestle with them, dance with them—sometimes while you're pregnant, as well! They also make messes—in their diapers, on their chins, on your shoulders, on the walls, in the bathroom—that must be cleaned up.

Then there are the mental demands. When you're a mom, you have to think, think, think all the time. Think about how to entertain them. Think about what to teach them. Think about how to teach them. Think about what items you should pack in the diaper bag to cover any contingency during any given jaunt. Think about whether a certain television show is okay to let them watch. Think about whether your 3-year-old is ready for half-day preschool. Think about how you'll pay for it if he is. Think about breakfast, lunch, and dinner, every day. Think about what size winter coat your little one will need next year as you try to pick up a bargain at an end-of-the season clearance. Think about how to respond when the kids don't mind, when they do things you wish they wouldn't, when they fuss and fight with their siblings.

So how do you keep from burning out?

✳ **Keep resources on-hand to inspire you** and give you practical ideas.

✳ **Keep a "Kidstuff and Rainy Days" box** of books and magazine clippings of easy activity and craft ideas for kids to dip into when you're tapped out and tempted to let the television do some serious baby-sitting.

✳ **Give yourself a break.** "I allow myself to be away from my daughter in order to avoid burn-out," says Laurie. "Although I believe I am her full-time mom, I don't believe that means I am the only person who can give her the care she needs. People who work full-time outside the home need breaks in order to work more productively, so why wouldn't a full-time mom? I read, sew, shop, take a bath—stuff I enjoy—and feel refreshed and ready to be a great mom." To grab a break when you can't leave the kids with your husband or a friend, Sheryl, mother of three preschoolers, has a tip: "I take 'sanity breaks' when I feel like I'm about to lose my cool with the kids. With the use of baby gates, I have created a couple of places in my house that are off-limits to the children (the kitchen and the master bedroom and bath). It's nice to know I always have a place to go for a few minutes when I need to clear my head."

✳ **Keep quick fixes nearby.** Does hearing a certain song always make you tap your toes? Listen to it. Does a certain Scripture passage always make you see things more clearly? Put it on your fridge or bathroom mirror. Looking through your kids' baby pictures might help you recharge your battery as you remember how passionately you wanted to spend your time at home with them instead of in an office somewhere. Does a certain movie always make you

Pop that into the player now, sit down with a
wl of popcorn and paint your fingernails or
some puzzles with the kids while you have a
laugh.

✳ **Remotivate yourself.** Think back to how passionate you were about your new job when you first
became a stay-at-home mom. Looking up entries in
your journal during that time can help you snatch
back some of the motivation and enthusiasm.

The attitudes we can cultivate that help keep us
motivated in our vocation as Christian parents are
the very ones that can help us keep our tanks full as
moms.

If you're feeling like nothing more than a servant in
your home, remember that in God's eyes, a servant
spirit is desirable in a child of God. In addition, sometimes we've just got to pick ourselves up by our
bootstraps and keep going: "And let us not grow
weary of doing good, for in due season we will reap,
if we do not give up" (Galatians 6:9).

"There are days when I want to sling the yogurt across
the room instead of wiping it up one more time," says
Alison, mother of two preschoolers. "And there are
times when I take so much out on my husband. Those
are the times when I have to say, 'Jesus, remind me that
this is for Your glory. Your momma cleaned up Your
messes and wiped Your tears, and she did it for Your
future glory. May this runny little nose someday be on
the face of a man who brings You glory, too.' And then I
wipe up and go on with life, knowing that the blessings
may not be seen today or even in my lifetime, but they
will be seen."

What better way to re-energize and remotivate than to return to the refreshment that comes from drinking deeply of God's Word? Remember what Jesus said to the Samaritan woman at the well, who surely was physically and spiritually worn out from the cares of her life: "Whoever drinks the water I give him will never thirst" (John 4:14). May we never forget that His strength will hold us up, see us through, and lead us on.

Which brings up a final strategy for quenching burnout:

✸ **Concentrate on the fact that this is only temporary.** Remember, we are given only a certain amount of time with our children. We should embrace this time, hog it, enjoy it, use it, make the most of it, indulge in it like a chin-deep bubble bath that won't be so luxuriously hot or bubble-full forever. Because it won't be long before they'll be gone from our care. These days will be memories, feelings, ones we'll to experience again only through pictures, videos, journal entries, and teary-eyed reminiscences. As soon as we feasted our eyes on each of our squinty-eyed newborns, they, and we, began the slow but sure process of separating.

So as we make your way through these sometimes tedious days of life as moms at home, let's try to take a few steps back now and then to look at the big picture. We can consider the smelly diaper changes, sleepless nights, scribbles on the walls, and constant clutter of toys as a trade for the privilege of indulging in our kids' everyday lives. Because they do grow up before we know it! To God be the glory!

# stay-at-home, mothering: it's a journey, not a destination

Let us encourage one another.
Hebrews 10:25b, NIV

While I researched and wrote this book, my best bet for getting good answers about the subject was to head straight to other stay-at-home moms. So I ended up interviewing and talking with more mothers at home than I can count. I learned two things from talking with these women: First, although I inexhaustibly searched for Stay-at-Home Mom Extraordinaire, a woman so together and on-target with her attitude and lifestyle that I could formulate from her experience one

road map that would lead all the rest of us to domestic utopia, I found that each woman struggles to strike her own balance between expectations and reality, child care and self care, needs and wants. What's perfect for one woman doesn't feel right to another.

Second, as I snatched up tidbits of one woman's experience here and another woman's journey there, I began to notice strikingly similar landmarks each of us reported passing during our homecomings and home-stayings. As an objective reporter, I'm supposed to keep my views out of an interview. But as a stay-at-home mom, I couldn't keep myself from interrupting to put in my two cents: "Me too!" I would squeal. "That's what I went through! *I felt just like that!*"

Because of the compelling nature of a woman telling her own story in her own words, I decided that I had to include in this book the results of one-on-one interviews with three mothers who are at various stages of their at-home careers. Maybe you can identify with one or more of them. (Feel free to interrupt at any time if you have the urge to scream into these pages, "ME TOO! I know just what you're talking about!")

# in the beginning, every day is a winding road

Key words punctuating Cyndi's assessment of her first year at home include "ambivalence" and "struggle." But what many moms call the most difficult year of stay-at-home motherhood has left the former teacher with an inner peace that tells her she's where she's supposed to be, a sense of accomplishment about the changes the year has taken her family through, and an unwavering optimism about her days of mothering that lie ahead.

## CHOOSING HOME

Although she says she had always wanted to stay at home with Daniel, the former kindergarten teacher with a passion for her vocation had mixed feelings about leaving her "other" kids in the classroom.

"I felt like I was abandoning them if I didn't go back to finish out the year," she says. "[But] Shannon really took the lead in that. He said, 'I just feel that for our family you need to be home.' It was hard to submit to

# cyndi

**AT HOME:** 1 year

**MARRIED TO:** Shannon, youth minister, for 6 years

**CHILDREN:** son, Daniel, age 1

**BACKGROUND:** With a bachelor's degree in elementary education, Cyndi quit her job teaching kindergarten to stay at home when Daniel was born.

that because I wanted to buck it. But I didn't want to leave Daniel. I think if it had ever come to that, I don't think I could have done it."

## GREAT EXPECTATIONS

When she considered the day after day part of stay-at-home motherhood looming ahead of her, Cyndi admits to having felt a certain degree of apprehension.

"I've never been one to love cleaning house . . . I don't enjoy that. I do it, but I don't enjoy it. I thought, 'I'll just go crazy.' Of course, it was a real struggle because there was a real desire to be at home with Daniel. It was never that I didn't want to be with him, or anything like that. It was just a selfish part of me that said, 'What am I going to do all day?'"

"I think I thought it would be like [the] baby-sitting I always did. When I was baby-sitting kids, we'd make play dough all day and we'd color and of course he's not old enough to do that kind of stuff yet, but I thought that all day it would just be teaching him his alphabet . . . I guess I didn't realize how much other stuff there is to do . . . housework and just getting up, getting ready. It's getting up and getting ready, and answering the phone and putting a load of clothes in or whatever . . . there's just always something to do."

## PHYSICAL AND EMOTIONAL ADJUSTMENTS

Compounding her uncertainty and sometimes off-target expectations about at-home motherhood were physical problems that came on the heels of her son's birth.

"I had some thyroid problems after I had Daniel. I think that, plus some post-partum depression . . . made it really hard at first. I've always been very positive about it, but it was very hard. I would just lie around a lot. I didn't feel well. I didn't have any energy. I couldn't get up; I couldn't get around. I'd use up all my energy for the things I had to do and then the rest of the time I'd just lie around. I knew something wasn't right."

The diagnosis and treatment of her thyroid problem "took a load off my mind that there wasn't something wrong with me," Cyndi says, "because I had felt like there was something wrong with me. I wasn't loving being at home with my baby. I loved him, but I wasn't chipper and up making breakfast and singing as I cleaned the house."

But medical treatment didn't completely fix things, Cyndi says. Because she had been so sedentary while ill, she had gained back 15 of the pregnancy pounds that had melted off right after she had Daniel. "So that caused me to kind of be depressed, to hate the way I looked," she said.

However, joining a Bible study that focuses on obedience as the key issue involved in losing weight helped Cyndi pare 15 pounds and 18 inches from her measurements—a triumph she celebrates with reserve.

"Food has a real hold on me and it's taken a long, long time and a lot of prayer and a lot of reading the Bible," Cyndi says. "I have to go to the Word of the Lord at least two or three times a day to make it through the day and not eat everything in the kitchen.

"The part about being home has helped me more than if I was out working. I don't think I would have the time spiritually that I have had to be able to work on this."

## MONEY MATTERS

Cyndi says her career change threw a big fist in her household's finances.

"We cut our salary in half when I quit," she says. But because the couple had already begun to prepare for a day when she might leave her job to raise a family, the prospects for making ends meet weren't as unnerving as they might have been.

"We tried very, very hard while I was working not to live on everything that I made," she says. "We knew it was coming that I was going to be home . . . It's still hard, when you have it, not to spend it. But we tried very hard to save a lot and not live on that so it wasn't such a big adjustment.

"We had looked at houses, and when we looked, we looked in a range that we knew we could afford on Shannon's income.

"We drive old cars and there's always a worry there. I have had to struggle with driving older cars. I want a new car like everybody else, but . . . I have learned that when we need a car, the Lord will provide it in some way. He'll provide a way for us to pay for it, or He'll provide it in some other way. That's the way we got my car now. The car that I had driven in high school and college was getting to the point where it was going to need a lot of work. My grandmother passed away, and they gave us her car. It was not a brand-new car, but it was six years newer than my car was, so the Lord provided that. We know He'll provide whatever we need. And it's given the Lord a chance to show us that He's going to take care of us and be faithful for the decisions that we've made."

## LOVE AND MARRIAGE

Her husband loves Cyndi's new job, but she has noted some subtle changes in their household routines as a result of her homecoming.

"He doesn't do as much as he used to, as far as house cleaning and stuff," Cyndi says. "When he was in seminary, he was at home, and I was working putting him through school. He worked at night some, but he was home during the day. He did all the laundry . . . so now it's funny, I see him going further and further back on things. Which is okay now that I'm home. But sometimes I think he doesn't realize how hard it is to be at home. He understands the work part of it, that there's a lot to do in the house and all that. But I don't think he understands the emotional side to it, as far as how hard it is to deal with a baby all day long.

"He's never said anything like, 'What did you do all day?' But I know sometimes when he walks in and he sees dishes in the sink or something, he thinks, 'Why isn't this done?' He never has said anything . . . but maybe I just think he thinks that. I start giving all these excuses about why the bed isn't made or why something isn't done, and he doesn't ask, but he gets an explanation anyway. It's a guilty feeling on my side."

## CABIN FEVER

The toughest part of her job, Cyndi says, has been that sense of isolation and confinement that seems to be universal among mothers at home.

"The very hardest thing for me, from the beginning, was that I've been so tied down. It is such a major production just to go to Wal-mart . . . because you've got to get his bag, you've got to get his burp rag, you've got to get his pacifier, you've got to get his bottles, then you've got to get your pump if you're going to be gone very long, then you've got to get somewhere to pump or feed him. Sometimes I would rather stay home than try to do all that. That was hard to get used to because I used to get up and run and go do whatever I wanted to do.

"But now I'll get to where I've been here for three days and haven't been out. If it's not necessary, I just won't do it. I just don't run to the store anymore for just the littlest thing. That's hard . . . and I'm not around adults as much as I was.

"That's why Wednesday morning Bible study has helped me. It gets me out with adults, and it gives me a little break from him, even though I'm always real ready to see him at the end of Bible study."

"Plus, Daniel's getting to an age right now that he's getting to be really fun as far as being able to do things, so we can get out more. I'm getting more independence again because he's walking. I'm not having to carry him everywhere. We're getting out and taking walks, and we're playing out in the backyard."

## OUT OF THE RUT AND INTO A HOBBY

For many moms, going home provides an ideal chance to spend more time on hobbies. But Cyndi has found that area of her life to be a void she's had a hard time filling.

"My husband likes basketball, football, baseball, fishing. He has hobbies. But I don't really have any hobbies. I like to do crafts some, but crafts are expensive. All this time you've thought you could make it yourself, but it's twice as expensive to make it.

"I really think my teaching was my hobby. I enjoyed it so much, and that's why it was so hard to give it up."

Cyndi has found a way to channel some of that creative energy by creating, planning, and writing a Christian kindergarten curriculum. "It's a long way off, but it's been kind of fun to do."

Another hobby she took up, Cyndi says, is making baby food. "That meant a lot to me. Maybe it was a pride thing on my part, but that was just a real neat thing that I could do for Daniel. I wouldn't have been able to do it if I was working."

Does Cyndi ever have doubts about her career choice and consider heading back to school?

"Not as much as I did at the beginning," she says. "I get panicky about financial things sometimes. Or I'll think, 'Well, it might be good for Daniel sometimes to be around other people.' But I think it's a selfish thing sometimes with me. It's an 'I-want-to-get-out-of-here' type thing. But that's usually the time I can call Shannon and he'll watch Daniel that night and I can go do something. All of a sudden it will work out.

"Shannon is real sensitive, I think, probably more

than most. He really tells me a lot how much he appreciates me. He tries to be real sensitive to me and to be that encouragement that I need.

"So I do have doubts. But then I know. I know in my heart of hearts that this is where the Lord wants me."

## finding her own road

karen

**AT HOME:**
3 years

**MARRIED TO:**
David,
accountant,
for 8 years

**CHILDREN:**
son, Jared, 5;
son, Galen, 3;
and one
on the way

**BACKGROUND:**
Resigned
from her job
as an office
coordinator
for a marketing
research firm
just after
Galen's birth.

With three years of at-home motherhood under her once-again expanding belt, Karen has traded in her insecurities for self-confidence, her unrealistic expectations for preparedness, and her fears for faith. And she's earned every bit of wisdom and insight she's gained along the way.

"I wasn't completely happy in my staying at home until it had been a year," Karen says. "I was so unprepared for it. I'm glad the newness has worn off. I know what to expect now. I'm more comfortable with being a stay-at-home mom."

## CHOOSING HOME

"I had the desire to stay home with my first child, Jared, but because of financial reasons we just could not do that," Karen says. "My husband had a job change while I was pregnant, which set us back financially. We just never caught up.

"When I became pregnant with Galen, I told David I still wanted to stay at home if I could and when I got further along, we kept talking about it. We decided to see if we could live off his salary. We did that for about two and a half months. My salary went to expenses that we had to incur with me working, such as day care. We also used it for doctor's expenses to have the baby. So we strictly lived off his paycheck. We were able to do it and felt fairly comfortable with it."

So after Galen was born, Karen took 10 weeks of maternity leave, then went back to work for just three weeks—"all the time knowing that I was going to quit. I worked one week, gave my two-week notice, then I came home."

Karen's family reacted to her homecoming with support—tempered by a little bit of concern.

"My parents, especially my mother, worried how we were going to make it financially because I had always worked since we had been married. They were a little cautious about it because they were afraid there was the possibility of my having to go back to work. I think I was afraid of that too."

## GREAT EXPECTATIONS: SUPERMOM STRIKES AGAIN

Like most of us, Karen embarked on her new adventure as a mother at home with a suitcase full of great expectations: "I thought that my house would be clean, that it would always be straight, and that I would never be embarrassed if company came in."

But Karen soon learned her lesson. "That was very unrealistic, on my part," she says. "I learned that you just can't keep your sanity and do all the things you need to do . . . [and] spend time with your kids. Sure, I can get my house looking immaculate, but then I'd be so tired I would not be of any use to my kids, my husband, or anybody. You have to know where to draw the line. You do what you can do, and then stop."

## LOSING KAREN, FINDING FRIENDS

Staying home meant starting over where friendships and support were concerned, Karen says.

"Because I had worked for so long [four years], my friendships had revolved around my office. And the few other friendships I had were at church, but they were acquaintances more than friends. I really felt like I had no one at first.

"When the finality of knowing I wasn't going back to work hit, it was hard for me to deal with. And because I didn't have that friend network of mothers who were going through the same thing I was, and didn't develop it until after I started staying home, I didn't realize that what I was going through was normal. I think I went through a mild state of depression there. Not anything serious, but it was sort of like . . . losing my identity. I went from a working situation where I had my name, 'Karen Webb, Office Coordinator' to 'Jared's mom', 'Galen's mom', 'David's wife', and 'Mrs. Webb', when somebody was calling me on the phone to sell me something. That was it. I had lost everything I had self-esteem from."

To fill the empty place formed in her life after breaking away from her network of office friends, Karen says
she went overboard.

"I tried to do too many things at one time, both in
the home and outside too.

"I ended up with everybody calling from church
because that was the closest thing I had to an outside
outlet. People would say: 'Karen, would you do such
and such?' Of course, because I felt like I needed that
outlet, I needed to be around adult people, I was doing
it. And then I kept thinking, 'Why don't I have time to
get stuff done at home? Why can't I do this? Why can't
I do that?' Not putting two and two together, I didn't
realize I was overloading myself with all my church
activities.

"I jumped in and I had no clue . . . and that's the
worst thing you can do. I made a lot of mistakes at first.

"The first year at home I think I went through several different levels of dealing with it. It's one thing
when you quit your job and there's not a baby involved
and you start staying home—you don't have all the hor-
mones and all that kind of stuff. But when a woman has
been working up to her due date and she has the baby,
she's on maternity leave and she has the attention of the
new baby, friends are calling . . . And then a little while
after that, it stops. She's left feeling like, 'What do I do
now? I don't have my identity at work any more, so
where do I go now?' For me, it was getting involved in
church. I'm not saying that's a bad thing, but if your reason for doing it is wrong, then it is a bad thing.

"I got to the point that I kept taking on more stuff,
and I was tired, and I wasn't serving my family in the

capacity that I wanted to serve them. The list of the order your priorities should fall should be God, husband, children, then whatever else. Well, I had my 'whatever else' way up here at the top, just because it was so hard for me to deal with not having that contact with other people. I think realizing that helped. So I finally just had to quit doing so many things."

## FINANCES: FRUGALITY AND FAITH

Most women don't have a conversation about stay-at-home motherhood without including finances as a key topic.

"We're not destitute by any means, but you always feel like you need more," Karen says. "Especially in the beginning, we had to watch where our money was going. I couldn't just go out and buy a new dress if I wanted to. I had to wait. And that was really a hard thing to deal with because I had been used to my paycheck and being able to do what I wanted.

"I may be entirely wrong in my thinking, but I think I sacrifice more on getting me new clothes and new shoes than I would have to . . . and I'm more frugal on buying stuff for the kids, especially toys. We have to be very careful. Their Christmases and birthdays are not as big. But that's just as well too. They probably don't need all that stuff anyway.

"You change how you look at stuff when you don't have that extra money."

That shift in perspective about material things includes a focus on faith in a God who consistently makes good on His promise to provide for the needs of His children.

"There are mothers who stay home who do not share the faith I have, but I think that when you do something like this, you are stepping out on faith. It's one of those things that you think, 'here we go.' But there have been several times when we would write out our checks and pay the bills and then an unexpected bill would come in—the car insurance is a biggie for us," Karen says. "And we'd be thinking, 'Well, we don't have enough money in this account to pay it . . . do we want to go withdraw $200 from savings to pay it?' We'd be debating about it, and the next day we would get a check and it would be enough to pay that insurance. I don't know how many times this has happened.

"I really feel that if you have your priorities right and you're serving the Lord with your money, you're giving Him His share, He will provide for you. He may not provide your wants, but He'll provide your necessities. With this baby, we may not have everything we want, but we'll have everything that we'll need."

## LOVE AND MARRIAGE

Karen sees her transition to the home front as one that has enhanced her marriage and strengthened her in her vocation as a wife.

"One plus I see is that I don't have the stress coming home from a job that I did before. I am able to, on a lot of days, get supper ready and have it ready when David gets home from work. That's a goal I have; it doesn't always work out. We do it when we can. But we don't both have that stress. I can listen to more of what he is going through."

However, the career change also has brought a certain amount of stress to their partnership as well, Karen says. "On the other extreme," she says, "I don't have my own life. My own life just revolves around the kids and the house. Sometimes, if there's something really bothering me, it's hard for me to get past that. I don't know why that is . . . I guess it's just because I just don't have something else to think about, or I'm always here. If there's something that needs to be fixed around here, I think, 'Why can't he get around to doing that?' because I'm always here. I forget that he works, and it's hard to do that.

"Also, in the beginning I felt more accountable to David on how I was spending money because it wasn't 'my money' now. I didn't so much ask for the necessities. I didn't say, 'I need to go to the grocery store; can I go to the grocery store?' It was more about, 'David, I really need a new pair of tennis shoes. Is it okay if I go get some?' I still do that to a certain extent, but not in the same way that I did do it. I do it now more to say, 'Can you think of anything to spend this money on instead of tennis shoes?' Then I was more asking his permission.

"It lowers your self-esteem. And David had done nothing to make me feel that way. It was all brought on by myself and how I felt."

Having to work through the nuances of a changed—and ever-changing relationship—has been only a minor inconvenience compared with the benefits of being a stay-at-home mom, Karen says. She doesn't have to pause even for a moment before she begins to list the pluses of parenting at home.

"I love being able to see my kids develop," she says. "With Jared, because I worked the first two and a half

years of his life, I missed out on a lot of things. But with Galen I've been able to be here for all of it . . . the good, the bad, and the ugly!

"I don't know if you can consider this a blessing, but when my children are sick, I don't have to decide whether I should go to work today. That was a decision I had to make with Jared.

"I don't have to worry about doctors appointments with the kids . . . that helps me, that's less stress on me.

"Also, when it's icy I don't have to worry about 'Do I have to go to work today?'

"Oh sure, there are days when I feel like I'm the Wicked Witch of the West. There are days that I think, 'If I have to tell them to pick up those blocks one more time, I'm going to go bananas.' But then, when it's my child coming out to greet me with this wonderful picture in his hand or I go into Sunday school to pick them up and they say 'Mommy, Mommy,' I wouldn't trade that for the world.

"We have our good days and bad days—and you're going to have that with any job."

*a mom's heart's at home*

As an advocate for stay-at-home moms with a passion for encouraging and supporting others who have made that decision, Leslie has been able to draw on her seven years of experience to fine-tune and articulate some right-on-target observations about issues that face us all.

## CHOOSING HOME

The beginning of her stay-at-home career forced the former teacher and her husband to maneuver a few hair-raising turns right out of the starting gate. First, Leslie experienced complications with her pregnancy that prompted her to take a leave of absence sooner than she had planned.

"Kyle wasn't born until December, but I quit work in March and stayed home and played what I like to call the 'Delta Burke view of pregnancy,' when you just lie around like second base."

Then, when she was seven and a half months pregnant, her husband was laid off from his position with a defense contractor.

"My skills . . . were pretty much useless because no one's going to hire you when you're seven and a half months pregnant."

Their predicament worsened when Leslie's pelvis separated during Kyle's early December delivery. The rare condition left

*leslie*

**AT HOME:**
7 years

**MARRIED TO:**
Mark, who works in contract administration for the federal government for 10 years

**CHILDREN:**
son, Kyle, 6; daughter, Marlie, 4

**BACKGROUND:**
Former high school speech and drama teacher

242

her unable to walk without excruciating pain—she was literally crippled for the beginning months of her son's life.

"I couldn't go back to work even if I had wanted to," Leslie says. "If I had had a healthy delivery, I could have gone back to work within a couple of weeks.

"So we were pretty much destitute."

After about six months of unemployment, the picture began to brighten. Her husband landed a job with the local transit authority.

"But the whole beginning part, my step into stay-at-home mothering, was a little scary at first because there we were—we were really in debt, behind on all our bills because of the time he was unemployed. For me not to be working was really a leap of faith. But we went ahead and did it, and got on our feet within about a year.

## LOVE AND MARRIAGE

"I wish I could say that my situation was one where my husband was and has always been completely supportive but that's not the case," Leslie says. "It's been one of those deals that I struggle with. Mark's mother worked. I have always been kind of the lone supporter of this concept.

"My husband told me after we had had these discussions several times, 'I married you knowing that you were getting a career started. You appeared to me to be someone who was serious about a career.'

"We had never consciously discussed this before marriage, and that's something that I think is really important that people do before they get married. At least have that conversation and make sure you and your husband are both in line.

"We've had to work through that, and he's been on the slow road to discovery . . . now he's much more supportive. But because the groundwork was so shaky, there's still that little bit of doubt in the back of my mind that he doesn't support me. So it makes it difficult, and it's something I have to sometimes struggle with.

"And then when I became a supporter, an advocate of the stay-at-home mother movement, it became even more difficult because he said, 'Oh great, now she's really into it.' I think that it made it even more diffi-cult—for him to recognize that this is something I am committed to for the long haul and not just for a few years until the kids start school.

"We're still at that place where we're trying to make that decision. And I am not trying to stand against my husband's will on this. If he finds that we financially need for me to work at least part-time when both of the children are in school, I'm willing to do that. But he knows I am committed to being at home when they're home and I don't want them to have to go into an after-school care type of situation."

Part of the reason Leslie says she is so driven to stay-at-home motherhood is that she comes from a single-parent family and wants to reverse the cycle for her own children. Her parents divorced when she was 20, severing her relationship with her father and wreaking emotional havoc between her and her mom.

"It's kind of a sad situation, and I think that's part of the motivation for my wanting to be at home," Leslie says. "Part of the motivation has been because of the pain and the difficulty I've seen that resulted from a family that is broken. I want to do better by my children."

## GREAT EXPECTATIONS

While she was on medical leave during her pregnancy, Leslie geared up for motherhood with the fervor of an undergrad cramming for finals.

"I did a ton of reading," she says. "I bought everything I could get on child care and early childhood development. I wanted to be the only mother in the neighborhood, in the region, in the world, who had done her homework on her baby and who was ready.

"I got all of the magazines, too. As a teacher I used to do this in debate class: I set up files for topics and tore out the magazine articles and filed them accordingly. 'Bedwetting,' 'sleep patterns' . . . I've got all these files of articles from four years' worth of magazines. That's how serious I felt and how driven I was about making sure I did it right.

"I did get a whole lot of information. When the baby came along I felt like I had been informed. I wasn't as overwhelmed, I think, as a lot of mothers. But I created a huge world of expectations that were unrealistic. In hindsight I can see that."

Leslie blames those unrealistic expectations on often-quoted experts who produce a steady stream of "never and always deals" in an effort to tell parents what they should and should not do.

"You read that stuff and you think if you go outside of that, then you have failed. And you set yourself up for failure immediately because nobody in the world can meet those expectations.

"One of the things I expected most from myself was to never lose my patience or my cool with my kids. I felt . . . that I would never feel angry with my children. I would always have this loving, wonderful, doting, devoted attitude about being a stay-at-home mother, that it would always be fun, it would always be pleasant.

"But then I didn't know how to handle the feelings when it wasn't. I would feel guilty and start to feel like 'I'm a bad mother because I don't like doing this all the time.'

"There were days when I didn't want to do it anymore. There were days when I'd say, 'I think I want to go back to work' because it would have been a whole lot easier to hand it off to somebody else, and go away and listen to the sound of nothing for eight hours, or to the sound of adults talking instead of a babbling baby or two preschool children yakking about something you don't even understand or Barney. [It would have been easier] not to have to listen to that, to feel like a grown-up, to put on nice clothes, and to walk away from it.

"I expected it to be so much more enjoyable on a regular basis than it was. I expected it in the beginning to be like it has become now. And you just don't realize that it's not going to be like that for a long time.

"So there's a lot of anger involved that you have to work through and you have to adjust to. It's incredibly challenging. I was amazed at how quickly I got angry at the situation and, therefore, my child.

"There were times when I blew it and still do. But

I've learned, it has taken a lot of prayer, 'God please help me with this because this is my weakest area: patience and anger with my children.'"

## MOM ON A MISSION

Around the time when her daughter, Marlie, was 18 months old, Leslie entered a phase of at-home motherhood that she describes as universal.

"Mothers realize that 'I've been completely absorbed in my children for two or three years, and now they don't need me as much anymore.' You wean them, they start to walk, they start to potty train. They start to be more interested in their peers than in you. You've thrown yourself into this child by necessity for however long, and all of a sudden, you feel yourself not being as important or significant.

"I think every mom goes through it. I haven't talked to a mom yet who hasn't.

Leslie believes it's crucial to a mom's emotional and spiritual health to find ways to reach out to others.

"Because we become so involved in our lives as mothers, and we don't reach out to other people, I think we have a tendency to miss an opportunity, not just for personal growth and intellectual stimulation, but there is a very real spiritual aspect to this that works hand in hand with our mental health.

"When you help other people, you can't be watching and looking at yourself. You have to be looking at them. I think God asked us in the Scripture to help others, to serve others, because He knew that is a healthy thing to do."

Making ministry to others part of our vocation while we're at home also makes sense because "it makes us feel good about ourselves," Leslie says.

"Because of the monotony of what we do and because of the never-endingness of what we do, there is often no 'look-at-what-I-did' to mothering. For the most part, you don't get to see the results of your efforts for a long time.

"If you will just step outside of 'my life's terrible, what am I, who am I, I'm just a mom,' all of that negative stuff we say to ourselves, and do something that has some significance to somebody else, it changes your whole perspective on who you are and what you're here for.

"I think mothers really shortchange themselves when they are only moms. Even if you're going to homeschool and your life is going to be surrounded with your children, get involved with a homeschool co-op. There's got to be something you offer outside of your home to somebody outside of those four walls. It feeds you."

Most women need a firm nudge before they'll take her advice and get involved in projects outside their homes, Leslie says.

"Women won't do that," she says. "You have to drag them kicking and screaming to mom support groups.

"You tell them over and over again, 'This is so good for you.' They just look at you like, 'I don't have time.' Yes, you do have time! Just don't clean the toilets that day! Don't watch TV for an hour. Put something aside that's so insignificant and do something that has eternal significance."

# THE BIG PICTURE

Hand-in-hand with Leslie's openness and candor about the obstacles stay-at-home moms face and her enthusiasm for helping them stay the course is her conviction that God gave her the job of mothering Kyle and Marlie at home for a reason.

"Every single day is an opportunity for me to learn more about what He's done for me," Leslie says. "For one thing, the thing that so many moms who work miss is the intimacy you get from that day-in, day-out exchange with your children. That is an intimacy that . . . teaches us a whole lot . . . about God's love for us.

"If you're only spending about an hour and a half or two hours a day actually with your children, and then on weekends, you really don't get the whole picture of who your child is. You might only get the worst of your child, or you might only be getting the best of your child, but you're not really getting the whole picture of who your child is.

"God sees us completely, He knows us completely. I think being home with them has really taught me how God can still love me even though I'm not always very pretty, even though sometimes I have dirt all over my face—all the ugly parts of our children we have to look at and deal with every day, and yet it doesn't change the way we feel about them at all.

"We still just absolutely adore these children, these little people. And that is a lesson I needed desperately. I don't know any other way God could have taught me that lesson other than having me home with them.

"I feel very strongly that nothing happens that He's not a part of. I'm home because He wants me home."

Appendix B

*safety first*

Moms who work outside the home make sure the child-care facilities at which they leave their children are safe. We must do no less. In fact, we must take extra strides to childproof our homes, because houses, unlike many child-care facilities, aren't kid-safe by design. Here's a quick checklist to help you make sure your home is child-safe:

# IN THE BEDROOM

○**Y** ○**N**  Does your baby have a firm, flat mattress (no soft bedding underneath)?

○**Y** ○**N**  Is the crib sturdy? Is all the hardware in place and tightly fastened?

○**Y** ○**N**  Are the crib, changing table, and bassinet out of reach of window blind or curtain cords?

# IN THE KITCHEN

○**Y** ○**N**  Does the high chair have safety straps (and do you use them)?

○**Y** ○**N**  When you cook, do you remember to use the back burners and keep pot handles turned to the back of the stove?

○**Y** ○**N**  Are your household cleaning products, knives, matches, and plastic bags stored either out of reach or behind childproof, locked cabinet doors?

# IN THE BATHROOM

○**Y** ○**N**  Are your medicines and cleaning products in containers with safety caps?

○**Y** ○**N**  Are those products locked away from a child's reach?

○Y ○**N** Is the hot water temperature set at or below 120 degrees to prevent scalding?

○Y ○**N** Have you slip-proofed the tub floor?

○Y ○**N** Do you remember never to leave your child unattended in the bath, and to immediately empty buckets of water that may be sitting around?

○Y ○**N** Is the waste basket behind closed (and safety-latched) doors?

# IN THE LIVING AREAS

○Y ○**N** Are smoke detectors located on each floor of your home? Do you remember to change the batteries twice yearly? (Mark your calendar so you won't forget.)

○Y ○**N** Do you use safety gates to block stairways and steps?

○Y ○**N** Do you have all electrical outlets covered with safety plugs?

○Y ○**N** Are lamp and computer cords tucked safely out of baby's grasp?

○Y ○**N** Do you constantly scan the floor for small objects, including tiny toys and balloons, buttons, etc., that might cause choking?

○Y ○**N** Have you stored away wobbly or dangerous furniture that might tip over on a baby or child?

○Y ○N   Have you anchored tall shelves to the wall?

○Y ○N   Are houseplants out of reach?

○Y ○N   Do you have a cushioned guard around the fireplace hearth?

○Y ○N   Do you keep a fire screen across the fireplace?

# IN THE TOY BOX AND ON THE TOY SHELF

○Y ○N   Do you throw away toys with sharp edges or points, toys that are too small, or toys that have detachable small parts?

○Y ○N   Does your hinged-lid toy box have a safety lid support?

○Y ○N   Is the toy shelf safely anchored to the wall, if necessary, to prevent it from tipping over if your little one decides to go for a climb?

# IN THE YARD

○Y ○N   Is your swimming pool fenced off, with the gate locked at all times?

○Y ○N   Do you empty wading pools after use?

○**Y** ○**N** Do you store "water collectors" such as wading pools, tubs, large lids, buckets, wheelbarrows, etc., on their side or upside down?

○**Y** ○**N** Do you scan the yard for dangerous items such as broken glass, rusted nails, empty cans, etc.?

○**Y** ○**N** Is the swingset or other play equipment safely anchored and in good working order? Are there caps on all exposed sharp hardware?

○**Y** ○**N** Do you keep gardening/yard tools such as rakes, shovels, etc., as well as lawn chemicals, behind locked doors?

No matter how careful we are to make our homes safe for our children, accidents will still happen. So to be ready for inevitable emergencies, take a first-aid/CPR course. Check with your local hospital or the American Red Cross for information on classes offered. And keep your well-stocked first-aid kit and CPR instructions on-hand so you'll be able to deal quickly with emergencies.

Appendix C

# resources for stay-at-home moms

If you worked outside the home before becoming a stay-at-home mom, you probably had access to one or more professional organizations related to your field. These organizations served several purposes, among them offering you the opportunity to network with others in your field, helping you develop your skills through continuing education, and presenting seminars or meetings at which speakers motivated you to do the very best you could at your job. Your current career is no different. Although, the publisher of this book and I do not endorse them, the following resources for tools might help equip you for your job mothering at home.

## FAMILYLIFE

www.familylife.com

"That's *real* family life." You may hear this comforting tagline regularly if you listen to Christian radio; it's the signature conclusion to brief but power-packed radio spots offering advice, inspiration, and encouragement to parents. The segments are just one part of FamilyLife's ministry to parents and families; if you're not already familiar with this organization, you should check it out soon because the Web site alone offers an abundance of articles and interviews on every topic imaginable concerning Christian family life.

A division of Campus Crusade for Christ, FamilyLife exists to effectively develop godly families who change the world one home at a time. The ministry's programs and resources—including marriage conferences, Bible studies, and daily radio broadcasts—help define roles in marriage and give parenting suggestions.

For more information about FamilyLife, visit its website. While you're there, sign up for *The Family Room*, a free monthly on-line magazine with featured articles and updates on FamilyLife events.

## FAMILY AND HOME NETWORK

www.familyandhome.org

This 20-year-old organization, previously named Mothers at Home, has made great strides in advancing the public's perception of mothers at home. The nonprofit, nonreligious organization publishes a monthly print journal, *Welcome Home*, as well as other books and products, and its Web site is loaded with articles about issues affecting stay-at-home moms and dads. A particular strength of this organization is its efforts to seek the best interest of parents through participation in local and national government and by involvement in the media. Part of their published purpose is to seek "to make public policies fair to parents who provide childcare to their own children." Access articles on the website free; the subscription and membership in the organization require payment.

## FOCUS ON THE FAMILY

www.family.org

The name of this Christian organization says it all. Founded in 1977 by Dr. James Dobson, Focus on the Family is a powerhouse of advice and encouragement designed to preserve and strengthen our families. The Web site is one you'll want to visit often for information and inspiration.

## HEARTS AT HOME

www.hearts-at-home.org

900 W. College Ave.

Normal, IL 61761

309–888–MOMS

Hearts at Home is an organization designed to encourage, educate, and equip women in the profession of motherhood. Through large conference events many attendees call "mommy school," Hearts at Home casts the vision that motherhood is a viable career choice. In addition to their events, Hearts at Home provides a variety of web and published resources to encourage women in their personal and family lives.

## HOMEBODIES

www.homebodies.org

"Helping parents find their way home" is the focus of this Web site that features support and encouragement for stay-at-home parents in its articles. With a Christian perspective the site offers opportunities for connecting with other at-home parents and features an excellent listing of additional helpful resources.

## MOMS IN TOUCH INTERNATIONAL

www.momsintouch.org

An organization comprised of groups of two or more moms who, fully believing that prayer makes a difference, meet for one hour each week to pray for their children, their schools, their teachers and their administrators. Visit the Web site to learn how to start a group in your community.

## MOPS—MOTHERS OF PRESCHOOLERS

www.mops.org

PO Box 102200

Denver, CO 80210–2200

303–733–5353

If you've already read the rest of this book, you'll know what a lifeline the local chapter of this Denver-based, Christian program geared toward mothers of young children has been to me. With more than 3,200 groups in the United States, the organization also has a MOPS program established in 30 foreign countries. Check the website to find out details about the MOPS groups in your area.

# STAY-AT-HOME DADS

### SLOWLANE

www.slowlane.com

I'm only including a handful of resources in this section of the book that aren't distinctly Christian, and this is one of them because resources for stay-at-home dads are indeed so few and far between. The extensive, searchable site offers links and articles addressing issues of interest to dads who swap the briefcase for the diaper bag. The list of links alone makes it well worth your visit.

# WORKING AT HOME

### HOME WORKING MOMS

www.homeworkingmom.com

Features articles and information designed to help get you started working from home.

### WAHM—WORK AT HOME MOMS

www.wahm.com

WAHM, the online magazine for Work at Home Moms, says if "every day at your office is 'Take Your Daughter to Work Day,' if there are Legos under your desk, and if your coffee pot is the most used appliance in your home, then you're a WAHM."

"WAHM is for moms who are trying to balance a family and home business, and also for the working moms who are thinking about leaving the traditional workplace," says founder Cheryl Demas, who left her engineering career and became an at-home mom when her 7-year-old daughter was diagnosed with diabetes just three days before her younger daughter was born.

"WAHM is dedicated to promoting work-at-home moms' businesses, providing information about legitimate work-at-home opportunities, and providing tips, advice, and entertainment to work-at-home moms everywhere," says Cheryl. For more information, check out the Web site.

# FOR THE KIDS

### CRAYOLA KIDS

www.crayola.com

Don't want to get too commercial in this resource listing, but I don't think I could have entertained my kids through the years without stopping at this site periodically to download printable projects or to get ideas for rainy day crafts.

### EVERYDAY ART

www.everydayart.com

I have turned to this site, Everyday Art for Kids, many times to help kick-start my creativity when I have wanted to do art projects with the kids. It's designed for adults who want to inspire creativity and a love of art in their kids, and it's written by Carolyn Holm, art teacher and author of the book, *Everyday Art for Kids.*

### FUN SCHOOL
www.funschool.com

This site offers more than 800 interactive games and activities for preschool through 6th grades. Easy to use and educational.

### PRESCHOOL RAINBOW
www.preschoolrainbow.org

Yet another idea-packed site that jumpstarts my creative juices when I seem to be running dry.

# HOUSEWORK

The following two sites should give you all the information and motivation you need to clean out those closets and shine that sink. Each offers a (potentially) workable plan for getting—and keeping—your house clean and in order. (Fair warning: Each site does include a fair amount of for-sale merchandise, so get your financial resolve ready if your budget's tight.)

### ORGANIZED HOME
www.organizedhome.com

### FLYLADY
www.flylady.com

Appendix D

# scriptural help for stay-at-home moms

Are you overjoyed at the sight of your newborn's gaze? Overwhelmed by the sound of her incessant crying? Are you aching for companionship or yearning for some time alone? Are you so busy taking care of others you have begun to wonder whether anyone truly cares for you?

Mothering—particularly stay-at-home mothering—can take us down such a perplexing path that help from God is the only help that's certain to guide us and sustain us throughout each day. The Bible is full of His wisdom that applies to every situation we encounter in life. Sometimes it just takes a little research to find the verse or passage that contains the treasure of truth that can help us at the moment we happen to need it.

With that in mind, here's a quick list of references to verses to provide you with just the comfort, guidance, or peace you need as you shepherd your little ones. Please don't let this take the place of hearing God's Word proclaimed in worship or opening your Bible and studying on your own; God has wonderful things in His Word for you when you spend one-on-one time with Him. But if the baby's wailing and the pasta's about to boil over and your toddler just knocked over a house-plant, try to grab your Bible and take a quick time-out to "taste and see that the LORD is good" (Psalm 34:8).

*When you're . . . See . . . .*

**Afraid**
Deuteronomy 3:22
Psalm 4:8
Psalm 18:16–19
Psalm 121:7–8
Proverbs 1:33
Proverbs 3:25–26
Proverbs 14:26
Proverbs 29:25
1 John 4:18

**Angry**
Psalm 4:4
Proverbs 14:29

Proverbs 15:1
Colossians 3:12–14
James 1:19–20
1 Peter 4:11

**Awed by
God's goodness**
Deuteronomy 8:10
Deuteronomy 8:17–18
Psalm 8
Psalm 13:6
Psalm 46:10
1 Corinthians 2:9
Ephesians 5:19–20

**Needing direction
continued**
Proverbs 20:24
Jeremiah 29:11
Jeremiah 42:3
Colossians 4:17

**Praying for
your children**
Psalm 5:3
Ephesians 1:16–18
Ephesians 3:14–19
Colossians 1:9–10

**Seeking hope**
Psalm 130:5, 7
Micah 7:7
Romans 8:24
Romans 15:13
Hebrews 10:23

**Seeking peace**
Psalm 85:8
Proverbs 17:1
Isaiah 26:3
John 14:27
Romans 5:1
Romans 8:6
1 Corinthians 14:33

**Seeking wisdom**
2 Chronicles 1:10
Psalm 32:8
Psalm 51:6
Proverbs 14:1
Proverbs 24:3
Matthew 7:7–8
Matthew 7:24
1 Corinthians 2:7
James 3:13

**Weary**
Exodus 14:14
2 Chronicles 16:9
Psalm 18:32
Psalm 62:1
Psalm 91:1
Isaiah 51:9
Matthew 11:28–29
Mark 6:31
1 Corinthians 15:58
Philippians 3:13b
Colossians 3:23–24
1 Peter 5:10–11

**Worried**
Psalm 55:22
Proverbs 12:25
Matthew 6:25–34
1 Peter 5:7
2 Peter 1:3

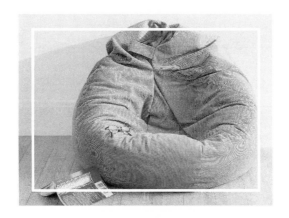

## Appendix E

# bibliography

American Psychological Association, *Review of General Psychology* (2001, Vol. 5, No. 4, 382–405.)

Stuart Briscoe, *How to Be a Motivated Christian* (Wheaton, Illinois: SP Publications, 1987.)

Fitzugh Dodson, *How to Parent* (Los Angeles, California: Nash, 1970.)

Suzanne Woods Fisher, "The Stay-at-Home Dad," *Christianity Today International/Marriage Partnership* (Fall 2000, Vol. 17, No. 3, p. 24)

Sharon Hoffman, *Come Home to Comfort* (Green Forest, Arkansas: New Leaf Press, 2003.)

M. Jean Soyke, *Early Education at Home: A Curriculum Guide for Parents of Preschoolers and Kindergartners* (Laurel, Maryland: Jireh Press, 1991.)

Miriam Stoppard, *Day by Day Baby Care* (New York, New York: Villard Books, 1983.)

Work & Family Newsbrief, *Wall Street Journal*, "Stay–at–Home Dads Have Re-Entry Problems," (8-26-03; accessed through www.findarticles.com).